ART

ART

Poems by
**Charmaine Papertalk Green
and John Kinsella**

Magabala
BOOKS

This is a 🐟 Magabala Book

LEADING PUBLISHER OF ABORIGINAL AND
TORRES STRAIT ISLANDER STORYTELLERS.
CHANGING THE WORLD, ONE STORY AT A TIME.

First published 2022
Magabala Books Aboriginal Corporation
1 Bagot Street, Broome, Western Australia
Website: www.magabala.com
Email: sales@magabala.com

Magabala Books receives financial assistance from the Commonwealth Government through the Australia Council, its arts advisory body. The State of Western Australia has made an investment in this project through the Department of Local Government, Sport and Cultural Industries. Magabala Books would like to acknowledge the generous support of the Shire of Broome, Western Australia.

Magabala Books is Australia's only independent Aboriginal and Torres Strait Islander publishing house. Magabala Books acknowledges the Traditional Owners of the Country on which we live and work. We recognise the unbroken connection to traditional lands, waters and cultures. Through what we publish, we honour all our Elders, peoples and stories, past, present and future.

Cover Design by Gene Eaton, Magabala Books
Typeset by Post Pre-press Group
Printed in Australia by Griffin Press

ISBN 978-1-922613-73-8 (Print)
ISBN 978-1-922613-766-0 (ePDF)

A catalogue record for this
book is available from the
National Library of Australia

Dedicated to my paperbark artist/storyteller Aunty Mary (*dec*) and my artist sisters Barbara, Catherine, Sheryl, Jennifer, and Caroline (*dec*).

Charmaine Papertalk Green

Contents

Data Sovereignty Words

This is my data, and
this is my Sovereign right.
No more whitewashing
Let *Truth* be told
Dear Australian Whitewasher,

Why do you find it difficult to understand 'my kind'
and 'my people'? Is it because of a whitewashed
Australian popular psyche? My kind, you know the
fair-skinned 'not real Aboriginal' kind. Yep, that is me
the fair-skinned one with a dark-skinned mother. The
one you tried to make feel different and displaced.
Sorry (not sorry) to disappoint but I do not feel
different or displaced from my Yamaji cultural mob.
I feel the exact opposite — strong, Yamaji, proud,
grounded, and defensively supportive of my culture.
You continually tell me in meetings, in media, in print,
online and in person that I should be grateful for
being rescued by your definition of civilised peoples
and a civilised society. You wrote and spoke that my
people, First Nations — Aboriginals — Yamaji, were
to die out and our culture and skin colour bred out
to hide many Australian history truths. I emerge
from the Australian mindsets of 'smooth the dying
pillow' and the 'half caste problem'. I was 21 years
old in 1984 when Western Australian Lang Hancock
mining land thief said, "the half caste is where most
of the troubles comes, I would dope the water up so
they were sterile and breed themselves out that would
solve the problem …". This was only 37 years ago a
white man's solution was to make 'my kind' sterile

not have any children and for my lineage to end with me. The intention was always about making 'my kind' disappear and making my ancestors' culture invisible and taking, owning, and keeping the land.

Therefore, I write /I protest /I talk/

I tell my story ... I am being me

Yours Truly, A Strong Surviving Yamaji Woman — Charmaine.

HANDS OF NULLIUS

And this all
started in the hands of nullius
resulting in Vox nullius
hundreds of years of
silence and invisibility

Data Sovereignty means
Telling our stories and
Putting our cultural interests
At the forefront of everything

VOX NULLIUS: NO VOICE

Yamaji had a voice
before you arrived
Because Yamaji was different
Yamaji was Yamaji
You tried to take
our voices by

Silencing Yamaji
Killing Yamaji,
Erasing Yamaji
Bleaching Yamaji skin
Through forced removal
Under oppression it is
hard to breathe and
Our Yamaji voice might
quiver and shake but
Yamaji voices remain to emerge
Through descendants like Charmaine

RES NULLIUS: NO ABANDONED LAND

Kurnell engravings,
shell middens
Evidence of occupation
Evidence of existence
Markings at the shoreline
Still a colonial narrative
Made Yamaji narratives
invisible and silent
silence

GUBERNARE NULLIUS / GOOD GOVERNANCE

Our Ancestors steered
The bark canoes across
The milky way for millennia
Our laws and culture handed
Down across generations
Culture captains like no other

People of the land survived
Under such great guidance
There had to be First Nation
Extraordinary governance

DATUM NULLIUS / KNOWLEDGE PLENTY

Travelling down the M1
I could not believe the
Way Mountains were
Parted for this highway
It made me think about
The way colonisers dissected
Yamaji knowledge and data
Cutting through Yamaji culture
Slicing everything apart leaving
Fragments standing on country
I thought about the Koori
Of this country I drove thru
Did those mountain tops
Hold rock engravings now
Erased or cut into pieces?
Or did they remain on top?
With everything else around
Removed by today's need
Isolated and not whole

Their colonials wrote
Their settlers wrote
Their historians wrote
Their academics wrote
Their western framework wrote

THAT

These lands had no history
Prior to the British arriving

THAT

Became the Great Australian Silence
A vision created by strangers

THAT

Curation by colonials
Blinded by western savage ideas
Ignoring in plain sight

THAT

60,000 years plus of history
They could not match
So, write First Nations out

BUT

Here we all are with our Yamaji stories

And there I was in my mother's womb gathering data.
I heard, felt, and experienced her life before my birth
— the happiness, the stress, the sadness, the everything.
Nothing could be hidden, we were attached to each other
so that I could survive. I was gathering data. All her emotions
and heartbeat flowed through to me in her womb until I
entered the world. I was gathering data.

CPG

Indexing

Indexing *The Land Selector's Guide to the crown Lands*
of Western Australia 'issued by direction of ... Commissioner
of Crown Lands' in Perth By Authority of the Government Printer
1897 you might realise absence and sameness, that real estate
advertising, marketing, and government approvals
to 'develop' are much the same, that being colonial
has many degrees as well as many avenues of denial.

A garden, a dwelling, the particular aims, hopes, desires ...
needs of the selector — orchards, root crops, transport infrastructure,
soil quality, size of, extent, locality are variables of productivity
for building economic communities with all their threads
and subtexts, paratexts, and separate indexes to separate
volumes. Resources. Sections. Extent. Agricultural districts.
Proximity to *The* Capital. Gazetting. Before and after surveys.

Approx. cost of clearing an acre of *such bush*. Well-watered
not so well-watered. Rainfall intensity. Lack. Compensated
by. Conditions. Worked. Blocks. Experimental Farms. Methods
improved, methods cropped. 'Mixed farming'. Opened for. Select:
cereals. It has been found. Has. Been. Found. 'by experience
that the cost of clearing lands timbered by salmon gums,
morrell, and gimlet wood is considerably reduced, owing

to the inflammable nature of those timbers.' Nature. Of. Those.
Timbers. See page. See megafires. Index error out on a limb. Future.
See: no woodlands not heavily timbered but crops and houses
and ... atmosphere flammable. Chain reaction. Cascade. Ghost
in the Hellbox. Cravers of holdings. Conditional. Balance
to be paid. Down. Getting their own clause in. Theirs?
Ours? Improvements to rip & tear, grub & burn. Maximum

persons per acreage. No person under eighteen
to purchase. Lend lease war talk later — building up
to quota, supply, drafts. Forfeits. Rentals and even freebies
as in Mt Bruce when on the bare bones had us consider
at least. Us. Them. Now payable. Within expiry
date. Or waived through landscaping
       the index.

    JK

On the Art of Shane Pickett:
A Visual Feast of Seeing

I stepped into the
Hay Street Gallery
A visual feast from
An artist shifting the
Layers of country and
Story into seeing for
Not only your eyes
But your mind and
Your senses jumping
Off the canvas towards
Or merging into the
Canvas and embracing the
Artistic feasts on offer
The artist's hands of the
Master of application
The energy maker of seeing

CPG

On the Art of Shane Pickett:
Celebration of Seeing

I look a long time,
then again, shaded
   from the hot hot sun,
   the night sky's
shadows or the frog
calling through layers
   of damp leaves,
   earth, streams,
to follow starlines,
to rockshift before eyes
   hear something
   they say — a map, yes?
a plan I might follow
a bit then turn back,
   flushed with reverence.

   JK

Mapping Culture Celebrating
(On Shane Pickett's Art)

Seeing is a celebration
of everything in life
not everyone can see
or have the gift to
bring stories alive from deep
within country and spirit
the landscapes,
the healing waters
the Balga grass trees,
the distant hills,
The fire and smoke
The morning dew and mist
The mapping cultures
Dotted pathways across
Country and held up
And held together by
the Dreaming from
caves and rock art
energy from seeing
moved into the artist's
hands and onto the
canvas to healing
seeing is celebration

CPG

You Might Expect in March
on Shane Pickett's 'Wanyarang Cools' (2004)

You, reader, might expect
that I would know this March
weather, being here mostly as I am,
but I don't. Not really. It's shifting, too.
Fronts that are curves become distorted,
Doppler radar echoes; parallelograms,
rhomboids. These cubist shapes
from a '20th century' that displayed
itself on traditional lands,
landed from far away, a reflection
of something that would alter
world's weather. There is better
science in the painting. It was
so much cooler last night,
and we all slept better here,
but the world grew more
and more restless as we slept,
and we woke to restlessness
and not even the cooler nights
will bring such calm of form and colour,
though it's still written in there,
across the languages of paint,
the deepest inner knowledge
the artist takes to the world
that comes into the world
that always was, is, should be.
For in this, I see the shapes
of breath — of our own
inhalations and exhalings,
but of the land's too,

and sweetest breath *will* come
  warm and cool again,
transpiring and growing trust.

    JK

A Different March

The curves of life
Cast a shadow over
Dark shadows of the
Land created and
Then uncreated repeatedly
Layered over ancient
Spiritual connections
Layered over forced changes
Bringing calmer light
I do not see that weather
Maps they speak of from
The abstract art before me
I peer into a painting where
A society slices culture
Like a pizza leaving one
Dotted visible slice to
Nourish and instil hope
For the custodians watching
Yes, ok I do think of
The weather but it is more
Ancestors' tears flooding
A canvas like soft rain
For someone else is
Trying to erase their story
But the mighty paintbrush
Of this artist pushes them
Back and for this the
Ancestors cry over country
in a good way

CPG

Dazzled by Shane Pickett's 'Three Faces of the Sun' (1986)

Where it closes open
end of each beginning
to purple hue the sun
call grow an edging
to centre a sunburst
to dazzle the spine
of vista and call sky
into its daily plan.

It's where the makings
start their ways, ignite
sap blossom limb claw
feather roost nest feed
welcome praise thanks
declaration for country
where you will learn
might listen to light.

Will be reached lilac's
yellow call its shade-
green unfurling fast-
slow all swept to flow
and join these faulty
separations my seeing
imposes on sun on skin
coming through paper.

JK

Three Faces of the Sun Dazzling

Just like the dance of rain
The sun kisses land
Every day and in everyway
Sometimes soft and gentle
Allowing us to curl up
Like a cat in the sunrays
Other times suffocating and
Forcing us to run for water
Or retreat into the space
Of air conditioners, verandahs
And comfort of shady trees
Faces of the Sun moves thru
The day at a pace only it knows
It is a commanding force
Controlling the paint palette
On display from sunrise to
Midday purples of distance
To glowing sunset warmth's
The sun determines your seeing

CPG

Through this Window I Imagine
Shane Pickett's 'Hillside at Dusk'

All strata held close to the heart
deep aquifer tapped by bores
but never drained by us, not now,
as it bleeds away the hillside.

This valley I square against
the house imposed under the echo
of sun, a residue of where it burnt
an eye into my looking out.

Offset the pattern of travel
to make landfall inland, the curve
of world, daylight cosmology
enfolded into close of day, encircling.

Still hoping for answers — tangents
to my looking — unasked for, matrix
stories by curves I cannot hear though desiring
nightbird senses awakening — right angles

of imposing this room. Land lives
above, below. Dusk knows,
my eyes weaken when interiors
are taken into firelight, everything!

JK

Shane Pickett's 'Hillside at Dusk' is everywhere

I live in Utakarra kinda flat country
A small ridge to the east of town
In the direction of the sunsets
And noise of semi-rural housing lots

I drive to wheat fields off Ross Ariti road
To catch the sun slide over this bushy ridge
I often drive to Geraldton beach front
To watch the sun going under the Ocean

Sometimes, I climb into the boats parked
In our yard to see over the now new
Annoying rooftops appearing everywhere
Most days I just need to see day merging into night

The warmness of dusk when land and sky
Blend into their shared space with colour
Like an ochre cloak bringing layers of
Rich colours in a never-ending cycle

Shane Pickett's 'Hillside at Dusk' is everywhere

    CPG

Should I Search for Personal Redemption Through Shane Pickett's 'Allowing the Glow to Shine Through'?

So much light and so little to see by —
I fear this might be true as I see one
horizon of hills and know another
beyond. But reading the land's shape

is not knowing the land, just knowing
the horizon's details, the universal laws
of sunset and sunrise. What makes glow
and what lets it shine through is hidden

from me — or maybe not hidden, just
not handed to me on a platter. I've
got to ask my way in, to look hard
and take away nothing more

than what I've seen before,
but be grateful with ways offered.
Should I search for personal redemption,
the sunset—sunrise glow feeding back answers?

JK

Shane Pickett's 'Allowing the Glow to Shine Through'

The soft glow of a campfire light
In the darkness of night on country
Allows an ancestral glow to shine through
A glow which is storied in many ways

The soft glow of the sun light bouncing
Onto the landscapes of our inner being
Finding its way through out to reach others
With glowing warm hugs and beaming smiles

The soft glow of a sunset sending light onto
The hillsides and hill tops way off in the distance
Making visible country that during the day
Was blended into and part of a bigger vision

The glow of the rising sun onto another day
Shooting a steady radiance of light for the eye
Splashing colours of ochre pink in the sky new
emotions of hope in a world needing love of nature

CPG

After Shane Pickett's 'The Tail of the Moon Marks the Land' (2006)

What trail can I follow swerving eyes closed
and cloth-eared to sense the flutter of night-leaves

as I cross where the moon has mapped
the vision? I only know what I can feel

in the map the story the artist has provided,
let me look out outside the studio or opened with air

produced on the canvas the page a campfire, on leaves
volatile in my head which I hope he'd be okay with,

but I will take nothing more than is offered
than by the conditions of viewing, of my

wandering without enough knowledge
to know every crossing the head and body

have made before the tail can leave its
brilliant encryptions, the lights of every

dance and commemoration, the sway
of treetops and rocks that catch memories

of every passing, every curve towards
the horizon of tomorrow. I can ask for

nothing but to love the touch of leaf,
of moon that is known better than

I know how, removing my shoes
to sense where it has been, the marks

it leaves — cool but sharp, a bite
soothing and possibly even venomous

and laughing, too. Laughing bright red
and yellow light of night's trails, footlights.

JK

Moon Tail Moon Dust

A slice of the milky way
Dropped onto and into earth

Wilara dust paints land

Like a magical paintbrush
Sweeping across country

Wilara light welcomed by barna

This painting took my breath away
Simply stolen by moonbeams

Wilara dust sprinkles mystery

I am sure the moon doesn't want
To be stared at all the time

Wilara tail light gentle touch

The moon wants to keep touching
The earth and sprinkling magic

Wilara dust sky memories

Into the song lines of creation
Through its comet like tail

Wilara light sprays into existence

I want to stand outside and wait
For the moon to bless the land

Wilara dust joins country to sky

I want the magical powers of
Moon dust to let me touch the moon

Wilara light heals all it touches

The way the moon showed the
Artist to make its presence known

Wilara dust and light belongs
And this tail must touch the land

CPG

Wilara is the name for 'moon' in Badimaya and Wajarri

Viewing Shane Pickett's 'To Stand in the Run Off Fresh Water Stream' (2008) and Wondering About How I Can See and Feel its Rapid-flow Depths

'The winning artist describes himself as a painter of Nyoongar lands and states in his artist statement, "In my painting I have depicted the power of these healing waters, pushing forth from the rocks, just like the power of the Dreaming that lies beneath all things waiting to be discovered by those people prepared to look closely and respect nature," Shane said.'*

What rocks will say, I saw water flow over and also
from inside out, trace anatomies, flow-steps across curves,
a permission to life? Making waves. And then intruders come to picnic,
to photograph, and some to bushbash, to block up the flow, to dig it out —
what permission can be asked for *later*? In retrospect? Always late, when
    it is before
the water mapped the shape of rock that sky spoke to surface, Respect!

Water across the feet is true now and always, and should be heard
and felt and loved, gurgling from where it has been filtered, held, released.

Go with the flow when hearing and seeing the streaming,
the burst of prism coming over and even out of the veins of stone —
watching for minutes and hours transfixed the flow
the flow coming back the next day sunup sundown
even watching the slow spill under constellations,
hoping to gain insight into the intramural
into the strokes of colour that land makes.
Stand refreshed and says thanks, thanks.

Water across the feet is true now and always, and should be heard
and felt and loved, gurgling from where it has been filtered, held, released.

I view with earth-foam at edges and yet have limited access —
the inside of the marble the swirling glass world
the eye of the sun the deepest part of earth
stories I know are to be held in awe when
the mines destroy and the fresh water
pushes up against them invigorating nature, defying.
Run off fresh water off the face of rock the natural catchment. Wonder!

JK

* https://www.deadlyvibe.com.au/2009/10/wa-artist-wins-peoples-choice-award

Fresh Water Running Healing Water

Walking into flowing waters brings a sense
Of healing to the spirit, body, and mind
The smooth rocks embedded into the riverbed
Have been kissed by water energy for many years
The moving sand particles makes a natural sandpaper
Flowing waters churns sand and water into white foam

The riverbed caresses our jina with flowing waters
It is the country healing, water and life moving together

Every colour of country from orange ochre to sunburnt brown
Mixing together in the water runoff and energy movement
Drawing out the toxicity of living away from not seeing
A water healing outside of the manmade spa treatments
The Dreaming through country offers the believer nature's
Gifts of healing and a calmness as smooth as the river rocks

The jina in the riverbed talks with the flowing waters
It is the country healing, water and life moving together

CPG

When I am Feeling Lost I Will Remember Shane Pickett's 'Red Tailed Cockatoos in the Summer Day (Bunuroo)' (2003)

When I feel lost I will remember
a ray of sun in season's heat & dry
knowing sparks of tails that can tell me.

I am lost in the tail-fire in the corona
of flock and flight and am grateful
to be swept up as leaffall glimmers.

Soon, the red-tails will settle and unpick
and make the next cycle — listen
to them flying in, letting you out of yourself;

I see them coming over the hill
sometimes, clustering, splaying feathers,
each one as great as the sun, following

trails I can't see. Smaller flocks
now, and a greater feeling of loss
I feel I should keep to myself, lost.

    JK

'Red Tailed Cockatoos in the Summer Day (Bunuroo)' (2003)

Redtail drags a ribbon of hope
Similar to when good spirits
Enter a space, everything makes sense
Totem handed down the line
Ancestor spirits returning to see
Showing themselves to calm down
Their people on their country
I heard them say "my old people"

Redtail drags ribbons of authority
Commanding a staunch presence
Signifying leadership high above
There can only be good from seeing
Majestic spray of colour like the
Sky is on fire and the connection
To country safely tucked away
Engulfing one into belonging

Redtail drags ribbons of water
Before it arrives to nourish the
Land and everything connected
A kinship not easily explained
By the unknowing moving on it
A parched land at sunset or sunrise
Awaits the arrival of life's blood
The Redtail messenger continues cycle

CPG

I See a Dugite and Know I Will Look to Shane Pickett's 'The Dance of the Brown Snake (Dugite)' (2004)

The top road is a bitumen loop that cuts
the brown snake's own swerve-path — to this dugite

I am staid, and have no access to the dance,
and nor should I, but I can see the swerve

across bitumen and then into red-brown dust,
looking into the red far behind the eye, into

the blue reflection of a bare sky but for one cloud
in its scales. I have always been okay around snakes,

and though I know people who have died
from dugite bites, I don't fear them at all,

and love the spirits of the lost people
and the eternal history of dugite, equally.

I see how to read the dance of the snake
is offered in the gift of an image, but I take

no steps from it — just a sharing of trails
like a long thin strip of bark blowing fast

across the land in front of me, caught in an easterly,
moving away. Not wanting my company, not really.

So, no ancestral knowledge, but a familiarity
with dugite crossing paths, knowing

how to let go and learn from its passing,
the moves it shows me, but not its story.

JK

Brown Snake Nyumbi — Dance/Shake a Leg

I stare in awe at this painting and understand
That the brown snake's nyumbi across country
Can make people freeze or shake a leg nervously?
Yet it means no harm as it belongs to where it moves

Brown snake dugite dance
                  Dugite brown snake nyumbi

Urban sprawl has not conquered the brown snake
Country is still Country and it will move across the
Land through golf courses, sand dunes and fields
Around houses and under concrete slabs dancing

Brown snake dugite dance
                  Dugite brown snake nyumbi

There is no brown snake beginning or end if you
don't know how to read the dance tracks passing by
where did it come from and where is it going?
Not connecting an ancestral spirit moving through

Brown snake dugite dance
                  Dugite brown snake nyumbi

The head is small but big and dangerous in its bite
See the big head and large orange eye watching
As if ready to spring dance off the canvas into life
The brown snake dugite aggression only provoked

Brown snake dugite dance
                    Dugite brown snake nyumbi

    CPG

On Shane Pickett's 'Hidden Marks in the Rock Face' (2008)

Where the trail ends is where it begins, the swirling story,
and while all of us can take our stories to the viewing,

it's not all our stories. All our stories are not the story
of the 'hidden marks in the rock face', though it might

be someone nearby's story as well. I'd like
to say, to look is not to take, and that healing

is the rock ageing as it needs to age. I know
there are said to be some viewers who don't

'have a political bone' in their bodies, but
I wonder what they detect where the trail ends,

and where it picks up and if that picking up
is picking up again? So *another* viewer might

say, The truth is in the burnt sunset the night
closing in till stars become beacons to the past.

I might listen harder without being intrusive,
without eavesdropping, but I know it'd be

art-talk, trying to find a way in. I accept
I have no way in but I have awe at the face

hidden in the rock face, and the family
and community conversations that go on

behind all that we can see on display,
deep inside the marks some of us can't see —

light comes from everywhere, so does darkness,
and there's a story there lighting the ways.

JK

Rockface Narratives

The rockface narrative carries with it culture
Our ancestors and old people always watching

Have you ever been in a car driving towards a
Rockface and have said "look at that old man's face"?

Or said, "I can see old people in that rockface."
I know many Yamajis who say this all the time

It is true the hidden message can always be found
When country has a face larger than life reminding

In this painting 'Hidden Marks in the Rock Face'
I see a woman with a baby on her back and

Her story may have ended or is just beginning
But her journey path is certainly a long one

Dotted across country in a flowing pattern but
Staying on a sunburnt path of an ochre sunset

I wonder what her story is and what part of country
Is her belonging, and where are her people now?

It is true rockfaces have hidden marks carrying messages
Through larger-than-life face shapes or body shapes

Or belonging to narratives and stories of country
Just resting to be told or just watching over protecting

CPG

Asking Permission to Connect With Shane Pickett's 'On the Horizon of the Dreaming Boodja' (2005)

I fell into the lines of this horizon
years after sunset maybe not so long after
its composition, and gasped — I risked
seeing through where I was born,

where I walked, where I have drawn
most of my breath, and I risked
understanding part of it via
Mark Rothko's answer in horizontals

in quadrilaterals but the paths are
otherwise. Can we implicate the life
of a Latvian Jewish American in an
encounter, through the overwhelming

specificity and immensity of country,
the corrective to colonial history
Shane Pickett's horizon offers?
Again, I ask permission and won't

take it for granted should it be even
granted, all this imposition of abstract
expressionism that Rothko declined?
No, each step each light is aglow

with so many and so much the Crown-white
control mechanisms would suppress
or show up only when the price
is right, when there's a profit

to be turned from country.
I disavow these profiteers
as I would like to avow
horizontals and verticals

and the winding paths
of starlight night
tracing the dark
events the distance

we walk to in sleep,
blowing out the light, the fires,
the white light which is of
itself, of its own creation —

a *dreaming* I know is there
but can't see in my darkness.

JK

Response to 'On the Horizon Dreaming Boodja'

I fell into the lines of the horizon from birth because
It is a way to understand direction and country story
Pathways were laid in the directions of the eastern
and western horizons when the sun and moon rose
And the sun and moon sets dragging the tidal waters

On these two horizons the celestial stories merged
With the culture stories and stories of country in a
Way that could not separate culture, people and the
Important Dreaming of everything into existence

I talk not of the dreams you have at night nor the
Dreams you hold about where your life paths go
This is not the Dreaming of country I see in this
Magnificent painting bringing to life country itself

I wake early to look out my kitchen window to the east
There the colours change as do the birdsongs
Around me, and I think about my ancestors who
Would have seen the same sunrise when they woke.

And when the sun drops into the western horizon
I check my windows for changes in the sky and
Cloud colours for the natural firework of pink and
Ochres splashed across the sky like a big canvas

'On the Horizon Dreaming Boodja' is painted in such
A way that it draws out the stories from within you
There is an ethereal feeling radiating across the
Horizons belonging to everyone looking in and
Saying 'You are beautiful and so is your country'.

CPG

Shane Pickett's 'Morning Clouds and a Warming Day'

Up with the hope that morning will
open my senses will replace

a sleepless night and smother
doubt with a low-high cloud mix

billowing from the agitated ocean
inland over ashen stretches to say

something I should listen to, or, if part-made
locally over chipped and rubbed hills,

to add to the meagre knowledge
I have, storing up to share

a way back to where I've never
been and maybe can't or shouldn't

go — a refrain of fact. But I am in this making
my own way because heat is hastening

and the warming morning is still kind to us
and to the day no matter how threatening 'later'

might be — always giving something
first before it becomes harsh, but I am

unable to sense completely out-of-doors
from inside the house from what I've had

handed to me as tools to see (legacy,
school, the social structures I've tried

to hide from), and smell and taste
and rub fingerprints as evidence

against the granite and clay and dust surfaces
of day, saying, It's so humid *but* dry, and seasons

won't resolve the sun, though, in-part,
that's my inability to pick out

the patterns older and sturdier directions
than global capital and the imperial

dregs of survey enforce, for I find redness
becomes bleakly silent in my scraping up

against twigs and glassy-sharp leaf-tips
finding my way through textures

of morning clouds warming day
which has so many words for so

much so inclusive and particular
and my poetry is limited as a greenhouse

the failed weather report
though I do know what's likely

to fly in to bloom and open
but to what ends I will

search the bandwidths of land
and its test pattern of intimacy,

admire the speech of redness
so eloquent and devastating

and not letting morning
go unclouded from what is held-

in over the dryness, warming
further and further — letting

us know if we'll take note. Speak.
Record our journey out of morning.

    JK

Response: Shane Pickett's 'Morning Clouds and a Warming Day'

At sunrise the morning cloud
throws colours of the sun out

To those waking into another
hot day bringing a sense of

Relief and perhaps joy for those
without pumping air-conditioning

Or cooling wind pushing past
inland for everyone to feel

Some time ago I drove across
the nullabor a few times and

Driving into a warming day
was felt through the car window

Yet we counted the kangaroos
sitting under the tree shades or under

Some really low shrubs watching
the cars moving past spreading fumes

The morning clouds so beautiful
out there with all the colours

Whilst moving across the sky
and can trick you into thinking rain

Sometimes I think the morning clouds
is better than the weather person

on television, just look at the
clouds to see the heat coming

After a red-hot day with a small fan
the nights can be just as red-hot

With the streams of restlessness
and many trips to the shower

To cool down especially in that
Pilbara heat inside a fibro home

This painting reminds me of that
red dust and hot energy onto land

This painting reminds me of a
Childhood below the 26th parallel

In Western Australia when the
social housing criteria did not

include fans for cooling down people
ice blocks from the trains were taken

And then in the recent heat waves in
Geraldton with power outages causing

The hot temperature to creep inside homes
Destroying food and pushing emotions hot

The morning clouds on a warming day
Brings a sense of energy to move forward

The morning clouds on a warming day
Brings a sense of relief even though not rain

This painting reminds me of a time
at Boolardy Station on an art trip

with Yamaji Art and scientists together
And it was 50 degrees yet the film crew

still wanted a big fire for yarning around at
night for the effects with the clouds rushing past

Then the morning clouds at sunrise was one
Magnificent sight before another warm day

CPG

On Shane Pickett's 'Guardians of the Good Energy Spirit' (2005)

Awesome!

Even if you are not privileged to see them
you might *know* they are there — sense
their presence even if you don't have
the spiritual knowledge and sensitivity
to know goodness must be looked over,
protecting against the rapacious and destructive
forces that take and then give just a little
bit back 'for the good of'; the guardians are rain
in the drought we all share, caught
in the making and the patterns of old
interacting like weather fronts with good hills
and good deserts and good rivers and good boulders
and good plains and good creeks and good forests
and good swamps and good seas and good reef
and good gorges and good stony places and good caves
and good lagoons and good outcrops
the good energy on the curve of the trails
across world, or maybe the volatile oil energy
of foliage around seasons that are shifted against
the embodiment, the orange smoke
of eternal sunrises, eternal sunsets.

Awesome!

   JK

Barndi (good)!

Goodness is offered in many different ways
And can be found in the most unusual ways
But generally when we value our connection to
Everything we touch, see, feel, taste, and experience

Barndi (good)!

Good energy guardians bring wildflowers to a
Harsh country to cloak its body and face
Bring smiles, cameras and a happy feeling out
Before heading into the heat of a glaring sun season

Barndi (good)!

Good energy guardians bring water to fill the
Rivers with the laughter of families grilling
Their chops around the riverbank campfires
And a season feed of inland yellow tails

Barndi (good)!

Good energy guardians throw ochre into the
Early evening sky painting a sunset of smiles
Love, hope, and sharing of sunsets on Instagram
brighter than a red tail cockatoo feather above

Barndi (good)!

    CPG

On Shane Pickett's 'Hidden in the Grass Trees is the Fire from the Moon's Tail' (2006): a memory merge

I hallucinated fire as a kid but fire was really approaching
the outcrop where the grass tree leaves made arcs and lines
I was lost amongst, and where I was sort of obsessed with them,
using small bits of leaf to mark patterns on the ground, make things,
pricking myself with the sun-bleached points, link fragments
into outlines which I would fill with bits and pieces, all alone
in the bush wondering even back then how I could manage to be so alone,
and then, abruptly, fire *was* approaching and the daymoon got lost in smoke
and I never thought it responsible for the fire but rather a header-
blade hitting a rock and igniting a wheatcrop out past
the island of bush where I hid and tried to be lost from sight
and saw lines and splinters of light I tried to use as a way
out of perspective and having seen painfully toppled grass trees
with their matchbook-like segments exposed to daylight
I became suddenly so afraid I hid among the grass trees
thinking I could resist fire like them, could survive to flower,
and that tip inside the grass tree that implants that 'growth-point'
inside and below ground that is life behind the dead leaves
and the forever trunk and if I'd known then what is shown
in this painting of Mr Pickett's then I would have maybe known
to leave that place before it was too late and to come back
afterwards gently over the ash and learn more than I could
trying to illustrate without any stories without any intensity
of knowing the growth as a vast interactive array
of knowledge and senses, of images and movements
of fire that lives in the grass trees and is only seen
by those who know how to look, who see
the many different colours of fire, its growth.

And then I was inside a house surrounded by firebreaks
and water trucks, looking through a venetian blind
at the fire the nightmoon the grass tree deciding,
falling and rising, falling and rising.

  JK

On Shane Pickett's 'Hidden in the Grass Trees is the Fire from the Moon's Tail' (2006)

The celebration of fire through fire culture
Fire keeping whilst walking to each campsite
and thousands of years of fire farming existed
well before a box of matches landed on country

On Gunnadoo Farm once was Grandfather Grass Tree
On the hill overlooking Wilunyu country and many
A young child stood whispering secrets and little yarns
To this old wise one who held many stories of place

Gunnadoo Grandfather Grass Tree would have saw
The Yamaji people carrying their firesticks across
The Greenough grass plains and then through the
Settlers' wheat crops copping a whip lashing if caught

Every astral cycle the moon tail would swoop past
The country's grass tree, slightly touching the stalk
Like a natural lighter being refilled with elements of fire
For all First Nation fire custodians to collect when needed

And so, nature's lighter sits hidden in the grass trees
Refilled and refreshed by the moon tail's sprinkle of
Moon dust throughout the generations that's why
The grass tree is special and culture important to many

In Geraldton the grass tree is a landscaping designer
Dream and is placed at roundabouts and in the
yards of those who can afford such a native plant
Here they even are microchipped to track thieves

Nature's lighter sits inside the grass tree in a blaze
Of fire colour exploding in the vision of First Nation
People holding the knowledge of fire culture on land
Although now others just like the vision of beauty seen

CPG

On Shane Pickett's 'Yonga Nyininy Balga Boodja' (2004)

'Nature is honest and I try to bring that out.'
  Shane Pickett

Though not specifically speaking to me
I hear it being spoken, and have seen
this land torn up by machines and levelled out.

Even bumpy and creviced and ravined
ground is cleared, flattened, and graded.
Sometimes there are piles of grass trees
that are just burnt to get rid of them

and you can smell that resinous smell
that should be part of some other
fire cycle but is an end with no regrowth

in sight, on site, not ever. Dead flames.
Though some grass trees are lifted from
their ground *beforehand* and transferred
to urban gardens, maybe in a new suburb

a new bare block, the promise of a water-wise
garden roughly where the grass tree itself
once grew. Even kangaroos, fenced in first,

can be transported half-dead and full of fear
to some other area which will be cleared,
flattened, and graded *later*. Next stage. I ask,
how can the town planners and developers

and the realtors and purchasers
even contemplate this given
the essence of the light? —

the blue mist of orange beginnings
and ends, light inside and out, all that *it* says
and would say and will say to those
who look *where it is,* knowing its plaint.

   JK

More than Balga grass trees and kangaroos

In country and colonial landscapes, it is
Possible we might see the same things
With paintings offering a glimpse into
The way we think and value we place
On the natural beauty captured thru art
The colonial landscape paintings sometime
Contradicting the colonial attempts at
Colonising and erasing our stories out
The painter making First Nations visible
And existing on land even if just on a
Small corner of the canvas sitting under
A tree with smoke rising from a campfire
Or out on the water in bark canoes
Or perhaps standing with colonial chaps
Or at a corroborree dancing in a circle
With their world changing in front of them
Yet in this Shane Pickett's painting the
Artist offers a deeper look into country
And landscape of beauty, mystery, culture
And stories captured through colour,
Balga grass and plentiful kangaroos
In the early morning at sunrise feeding
With Balga grass trees dominating as they
Should given their importance to culture
With sweet nectar, medicine and resin gum

CPG

I Am Not Trying to Find a Way into Shane Pickett's 'Healing Waters that Cross Flows' (2008)

When the tree-ending dry
was interrupted by 145mm of rain
which fell in just 60 hours, cutting
new flow-paths across the valley
I thought of them as healing waters
beyond the erosion, though much
of that erosion came from housebuilding
and clearing and intensive grazing
from one end of the valley to the other.

In this, I feel I see the paths of water
in their own rights, but I am too easily
affected by the addiction to seeing
and thinking I can feel a painting —
as if the universal fuses with the local,
as if different cultures of painting
meeting is about viewing as much
as about creating. But I don't think
I can say this, looking from deep
gouge of run-off in the hillside,
the exposure of bedrock loam,
colours of exposure to rockiness,
towards night beneath the broken crust.

And ochre-orange nimbus of water
rush and whirl says something
as physics and élan vital, a crossing
the flows of my damaged seeing,
my damaging seeing, my thirsty
gaze which I recoil from as water

thrashes around granite sluice
of the valley I listen to, corellas
flying in pairs and triplets from
east to west, centring the flow
into the twilight which lasts
longer as I move down
with the flow, amongst
the vegetation and its descriptions
of healing I hope to hear, to visualise.

JK

Life is a Cross Flow — Response to 'Healing Waters that Cross Flows' (2008)

Sitting on Adelaide Terrace looking out at the rainfall
My eyes dancing between the rain and the painting
Rainwater continues to kiss Noongar country — Whadjuk Boodjar
Water dancing on the powerful Derbarl Yerrigan in the distance
My first thoughts are to honour those whose land I am now on
The buildings and fast-moving cars are nothing but white noise

*Cross flowing spreading through **my spirit**, my body, my heart,*
My healing, my layers, my life — cross flowing never ending

My eyes dance between the clouds and the painting
I want to jump into the cross flow and let the waters
Take me on a journey across country, place and time
I want to float on the water with my arms open wide
Staring up into the Milky Way at our ancestors' many stories
I want to be that flowing water particle bringing life and renewal

*Cross flowing spreading through **my body**, my spirit, my heart,*
My healing, my layers, my life — cross flowing never ending

My eyes dance between the rain receiving trees and the painting
Cross waters spread across country to touch what needs healing
Country — Boodjar, Barna — determines water's movement across it
Just like the energy it gives us to heal when we go *on country*
If you can see country's story or message with your heart, you heal
If you can have a yarn with country and receive this energy, you heal

Charmaine Papertalk Green & Mark Smith, *Unravelling Archives 1,* 2019
From Series: 'Alternative Archive: Decolonising Reclaiming Debunking'
by Charmaine Papertalk Green and Mark Smith (2019)
Poem: *Responding*, pp 72

Charmaine Papertalk Green & Mark Smith, *Unravelling Archives 2,* 2019
From Series: 'Alternative Archive: Decolonising Reclaiming Debunking'
by Charmaine Papertalk Green and Mark Smith (2019)
Poem: *Exhibit:* ours *is not 'ours'* [*'Museum Thief'*], pp 70

Charmaine Papertalk Green & Mark Smith, *Unravelling Archives 3,* 2019
From Series: 'Alternative Archive: Decolonising Reclaiming Debunking'
by Charmaine Papertalk Green and Mark Smith (2019)
Poem: *I Hesitate Before Entering a Western 'Museum'*, pp 75

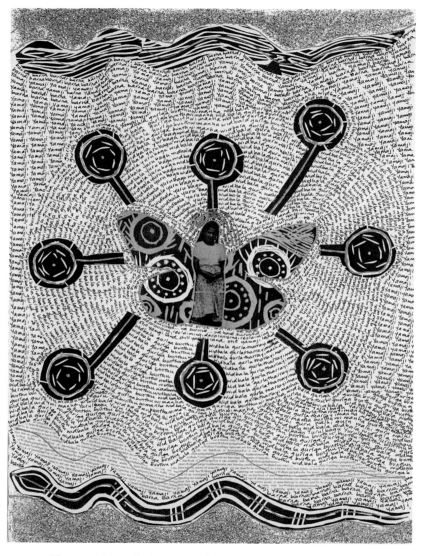

Charmaine Papertalk Green & Mark Smith, *Unravelling Archives 4,* 2019
From Series: 'Alternative Archive: Decolonising Reclaiming Debunking'
by Charmaine Papertalk Green and Mark Smith (2019)
Poem: *I Mentally Travel from Coondle to Geraldton and Think of the Survivors
and Speak Respect to their Country*, pp 74

Charmaine Papertalk Green, *Wildflower Time,* 2015
Poem: *Everlastings (2020) (2021)*, pp 97 – 100

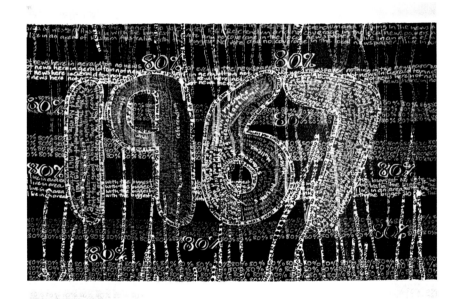

Charmaine Papertalk Green, *High Vote of No,* 2017
Poem: *1967*, pp 88 – 93

*Cross flowing spreading through **my heart**, my spirit, my body,*
My healing, my layers, my life — cross flowing never ending

My eyes dance between cloud breaking blue sky and the painting
This moment reminds me of just how complex the cycle of life really is
But where there is a beginning there is an end and they always meet up
That is what we call the cycle of life and that is why we say everything
Is connected to each other from the sky, the country, the waterways
This connection and relationship dotted across country guiding the way

*Cross flowing spreading through **my healing**, my spirit, my body, my heart,*
My layers, my life — cross flowing never ending

My eyes dance between the birds flying across the cloudy sky and the
    painting
The deep connection between water and healing is a strong cultural
    belief
There is something beautiful about water sources such as rain,
    waterholes, rivers
There is strong spirituality through our water stories and cultural
    practices
We extend our energy and respect when offering sand or leaves to water
    sites
We receive energy and blessings from washing our new baby in rock
    water pools

*Cross flowing spreading through **my layers**, my spirit, my body, my heart,*
My healing, my life — cross flowing never ending

My eyes dance between the white noise of buildings, roads, cars and signs
The rain has gone, and the clouds parting with white noise sounds lifting
I start thinking about intergenerational trauma and the pain washing over
Communities, ancestors, children, families, mothers, fathers, country
Then this painting makes me understand the healing powers and energy
of water
Touching every layer of our very being there is no flow pattern there is
cross flow

*Cross flowing spreading through **my life**, my spirit, my body, my heart,*
My healing, my layers — cross flowing never ending

CPG

On Shane Pickett's 'Moonlight Medicines and Healing Waterfall' (2008)

I don't go near stars that aren't mine.
I don't get near their stories and origins.

I can hear the moonlight plashing
down the granite sluices in the valley

below and I see the reflections
of the Milky Way in the sheen

of rocks in difficult to get to places.
I am sad as I study the pattern

of your stories again, and can't help
looking for medicine which is a splash

of red from galactic fusion, and I make sequences
which might do me some good, or I might

just be taking a placebo while the real
healing is to leave off searching

for a cure for myself and let the stars heal night,
cure daylight, guide their followers.

I can't go near stars that aren't mine.
I won't get near their stories and origins.

    JK

Moon and Water Healing

The moon fascinates when it shines so bright at night
Waking up the land in an ethereal way that even the

Birds don't sleep and those who are afraid of the dark
Can feel a healing and comfort in this moon light

The stars belong to no one and yet they can belong to all
A personal star story can be wrapped around your neck

But don't steal cultural star or moon stories from others
Because the sky world is generous and offers the night sky

With its jewellery box of sparkling lights lifting the spirits
In a dotted line straight through to the eye of the receiver

And on earth when the night sky overwhelms then look
For still waters capturing the reflection from above

Shane Pickett's 'Moonlight Medicine and Healing Waterfalls'
Reminds that night darkness is not to be feared because

The moon dust, moon beams and moon rays are the healing
Like waterfalls dropping down soft ways onto country while

We sleep and capture the dreams of our ancestors sent to us
As gifts so that we can dream for our descendants' healing

    CPG

Shane Pickett's Painting Is Very Real in My Life

On the wall of *Admissions*, 'Spinifex Gold and Pilbara Red'.
Yes, I think that was the title. It was one of the Pilbara
paintings, but *later* … in style, in reaching into where
things continue? So many different aspects of presence.
I was sharpish when I studied it early this morning,
but since then I have become hazy. And I am not
supposed to make crucial decisions during the next 24 hours.
I am still under the influence of anaesthetic, and everything
I see is a painting. I fixated on the ceremonies against
the trees laid as signs of water in the dry, their sheen
against the markings of country. I remember, this
is how I looked at the painting, not searching
because searching felt wrong, but reflecting
over truisms. It helped me find a way through
the forgetting of 'going under', and I woke
to the forms of roof, windows, ventilation
grids, smoke detectors, recessed light fittings.
It was all a matter of tenses, of temporality.
I thought I could hear a gold wind through
a red place and I was so much further south.
How can I be anything but grateful for such repair?
I am not saying I deserve it, but I am grateful.

JK

CODA — looking at Byron Pickett's 'Descendants' (1987)

Looking long at Shane Pickett's photo-screenprint of Byron Pickett's
    'Descendants' (1987)
and reading the pained words and the declaration of pride that are lines
    that travel
beyond any critical rendering, that are the essence of a painting in the time
of address and revelation, of the anguish and distress of finding justice,
I realise that the neck-chained Aboriginal initiated men in the background
which is not background of a scene but an always presence an always
pain, I realise that those men are the men that were in that large photo
on the wall of the hotel opposite the railway station, the one
I tried to remove from the wall, the one where I cried over the crime
of its existence, of it being displayed as a statement of claim,
the emptiness of survey and land grants and lies of voting,
and was beaten and punched over saying that it was so wrong
to display as trophy in the bar and the police dragged me
to the Horseshoe Bridge police station, crossing of the newels
with swan lamp bases, that mockery of country that progress of regress,
and kicked my head in because they, the constabulary, were having
none of that shit from a drunk a white betrayer drunk who at that stage
had never heard the expression 'white saviour myth' and knew
nothing of anything but the welcome lived by in the city parks
and the lines of beds in the halfway house where drying out
was possible. The couple sitting at the front of this screenprint
are beautiful people and I ask forgiveness for the crap person
I was in my failures in my inability to sort injustices so caught
in my addictions, and the crap soul I lug around with me still.
And I say the sum is truth and the stories you know and ascend
and descend and ascend are beyond anything I will ever know
and I can't say anything else and apologise for this as well,
this looking and drawing myself in where I fit in a way

I don't want to think about, but should. Those metal
swans on the bridge — representative art,
loss of swanness? The powerful presence
of Shane Pickett's artwork — its truths.

JK

Response to CODA — looking at Byron Pickett's 'Descendants' (1987)

Reflecting on this painting I can see a proud couple who
Like many Aboriginal people wear the colonial acts
Of much cruelty passed through intergenerational stories.
Intergenerational trauma and yet they still sit at the front
This painting evoked the memory a photo hanging in
Mum's house in Mullewa and Geraldton of a group of
Aboriginal men standing with chains around their
Necks and ankles whilst the coloniser stood next to
Them as if he was showing off some colonial trophy
I often wondered why Mum was displaying this photo
Of colonial cruelty, cultural pain and the sadness evoked
The picture remained with Mum until her passing and
Now it sits in a box waiting for its next moments
I seen the pain and sadness in Mum, and I think it may
Have been as a reminder to her, her family and everyone
Who would look at the photo of the Butterabby Graves,
Just 10 kilometres south of Mullewa at Devils Creek
A site where 5 Yamaji men were taken to be hung
We would go out there and clean up Butterabby Graves
To remember what had happened and the way all the Yamaji
Were rounded up as a reminder of punishment to them if
They continued to steal from and kill an invader on their country
My brother Charlie would write down their names and talk about
These men all the time from being caught, sent to south Fremantle by
Ship, and sent back in a ship after sentencing to Geraldton and
Then walked across country from Geraldton to Devils Creek and
The hanging site which stands today as a tourist site off a lonely
Road between Mullewa and Mingenew. I remember one time Mum
Started crying out at Butterabby Graves she just said "I can see all
My people standing way over there looking". That was a very sad

Moment that stayed with me forever. We all headed home that day feeling
Very sad for the Yamaji men and for the treatment back then of our people
All over Western Australia this way. It is a part of Western Australian history
That should not be forgotten. This painting evoked that memory of the
Following Yamaji men being hung on 28th January 1865:

Rest-In-Peace
Garder, Wangayakoo, Yourmacarra, Charlacarra, Williacarra
Not to be forgotten
Butterabby Graves, Devils Creek, Mullewa

We are all descendants with these old people behind us in the background
As part of our lives, history, stories, culture, lived reality and like
    Pickett's 'Descendants'
we have survived despite the chains of oppression, colonisation and Nullius

    CPG

Alternative Archive: Decolonising Reclaiming Debunking

Our data and knowledge are carved deeply into the rocks, caves, trees, rivers, waterholes, ceremonial grounds, night sky, artefacts, campsites, walking tracks, bushfoods, song lines, stories, dances, sacred places and our very existence as Yamaji. Our archives extend thousands of years beyond museums, libraries, churches and government records.

In the western world archives are generally viewed as manmade objects such as libraries, museums, books, fieldnotes, government records and so forth. These archives have been constructed for the western world through western patriarchy lens. These archives can and do create myths, for instance the "Terra Nullius Myth" and the "Hawes Myth". Our artworks interrogate both myths which have seen Yamaji become invisible in their own ancestral lands — creating conversations of visibility. The "Hawes Myth" passed on to tourist and church visitors alike that "Hawes built the churches himself". We question this and want to generate conversations of the local Yamaji and non Yamaji helping to build these grand structures on our landscape. Our narrative is to tell a story of reclaiming, decolonising and re positioning the nameless Yamaji who helped to build these colonial religious structures whilst being displaced from their traditional sites.

> *The poetry of stone /Belongs to not one man /To be worshipped /Like a bronze deity /Step lightly on that /Rock of knowledge /For it can crumble with lies*

> *Widbala /gurlatharrayimanha (ignoring not wanting to know) /Widbala*
> > *   /gurlgabunthu (deaf)*

Widbala /gurlga bunthuwimanha (not listening unable to hear) /Widbala /Guru walhi (eyes that no good) /Widbala /Yurulbagu (ignorant not knowing)

Then there is the worldwide "Terra Nullius Myth" of Australia being no man's land — empty and vacant for the taking is to be made visible for what it is — a myth created for the taking of lands. Our conversation is to keep visible that at time of invasion/settlement on these lands existed living Yamaji people with songs, dances, religions and a society swept away by ethnocentrism.

Our people have not /Been buried within /The memory of this land /For they exist through /Us their descendants /We remember and we /Will make visible for all

Yamaji /Malga garrimanha (standing strong and firm) /Yamaji /Wanggajimanha (yarning) /Yamaji /Nganhu thubarnmanha (we are straightening story out) /Yamaji /Ngurra Yungarra (One's own country) /Yamaji /Garrimanha (standing together)

We aim to reclaim the traditional spaces of our ancestors who had been displaced from their ancestral sites. We are from the Yamaji Nation with traditional connections to the Midwest and Murchison, and draw on knowledge and memory inherited from ancestors and journeys into western archives to decolonise and challenge.

Charmaine Green & Mark Smith, Yamaji Nation, May 2019

Exhibit: *ours* is not 'ours' ['Museum Thief']

response to Charmaine Papertalk Green & Mark Smith's, Unravelling Archives 2,
2019 (see colour insert)

I am not *(y)ours*
but I can see
the wrongs
of ways and
it doesn't take
much imagination
to take imagination
of annals to make
repository and
rearrange curated
'evidence' each
of us viewing
experiencing
interacting
each of us not
ours each of us
'our' own angle
as if we've every
right of opinion
but getting up
close and cosy
over the distance
of display of taking
in an impression
without hearing
the advice
the conditions,
and going back
to the colonial ways
of modern living

that are never
really 'our' own
but something
that happened
that's been put
to rights, surely,
telling ourselves
without irony
or self-awareness
of 'have you seen'
the exhibit
exhibiting
exhibition
of their *ours*,
while not connecting
the dots we know
how to talk about
it all with permission
don't we, learning
as we go but not
as we've gone?
Our permission
is permission
all the same
isn't it? Trauma
and reclaiming
and placing limits
where there were always
limits — viewers —
isn't irony
isn't a closed book
or a sign the guest book
moment.

JK

Responding

response to Charmaine Papertalk Green & Mark Smith's, Unravelling Archives 1,
2019 (see colour insert)

Sincere as cloth the complexity of the
Western subject the complexity of the
history of modifying by learning the
history of power around the loss of life
and the complete void of self-irony of
self-scrutiny of a humility outside the

Responding is socially acceptable the tenets of father the gilding
of sun, a and father and father and not seeing or cross-ways
manifold just denying or brutally administering manifest
vision of one understanding of knowledge and the 'book-
learning' data accumulated since incursion a few imposition
is compiling, years before or a few decades or maybe composition
and directions a hundred years while disrespecting or on how to
use failing to comprehend or just trying distribution
of data an to delete the files of millennia of excuse of
reasoned understanding of knowledge making subtracting
from what and recording of data in ways far more you have to
be replaced complex far more integrated into with what
will be dished country than all the systems of colonial up on the
cold cut plate export could ever manage or conjure the railings
to kneel the and pretend authoritative letting police, curiosity to
see the world government officials, priests, soldiers and and make
use of every- even teachers to force that knowledge thing see
those dossiers away to push it underground to crush of manners
and how to and replace it but hey, fourfold vision believe.
of the architecture of Western belief,
you failed totally and utterly and the
knowledge you can't reach resounds
and the data you can't gather keeps on

gathering in its ways its peoples' ways
and you have no access and your damage
is fruitless pointless obscene offensive
and a crime against the very humanity
you purport to save. The campfires
are artisan workshops and not the
factories that make products of spiritual
consumerism but maybe settlers
still don't see that?

JK

I Mentally Travel from Coondle to Geraldton and Think of the Survivors and Speak Respect to their Country

response to Charmaine Papertalk Green & Mark Smith's, Unravelling Archives 4, *2019 (see colour insert)*

Butterfly time, and I am watching names settle
on flowers as if the butterflies were a dossier
of colonial knowledge — common browns,
painted ladies, spotted jezebels, blue butterfly,
cabbage white … and I remember the moon
moth that flowered before the moon was up,
knowledgeable about the dark but also the light
that was going to spark behind the clouds.

All of this while I think of family travelling
to Geraldton today. I worry because the roads
are always dangerous and never predictable.
They cross from Noongar Boodja to Yamaji
Barna and I know they will be respecting
as they go. There is no one to look over
them and they don't expect it — how
can they? They are not the survivors.

It is warm enough now for the snakes
to be out. I hear that a galah glanced
off the car but was okay and flew
with the flock. They drive slow.
Between here and there the weather
shifts in many ways. *Weather
is not climate.* The records are written
in country, passing close, always remembered.

    JK

I Hesitate Before Entering a Western 'Museum'

response to Charmaine Papertalk Green & Mark Smith's, Unravelling Archives 3, *2019 (see colour insert)*

Western museums are not museums of the wild west but they might be,
mightn't they? I carry all my ways of seeing all my encodings and
    selections,
all my rejected divinities all my lines of poems strung out across the globe,
all my tracks through big seas under heavy skies, all my relaxing on the
    decks
when the building is becalmed. No, it doesn't feel like that in my head,
it doesn't feel like the me that I'd like to know, but something flaps
like a door not latched properly, the hot easterlies keeping things
on edge. I see a bit of moonrock or a meteorite older than a computer
and I remember the classroom on the day of the moon landing and yes,
there was a portrait of the queen. I don't know if that was standard issue
for the time, but being from a 'broken family' I knew that the teacher
intended the monarch's eyes to bore holes in me. The school was built
in sand on rock and it felt like it was slipping away into the swamp,
which was struggling to remain where it was. I collected things from
    around
the place — a seed pod, a piece of broken masonry, a plough disk, even
seashells — and started my own in-the-bedroom museum. But I kept
changing the labels — they never seemed to define the object they
    described.
Western museums are not museums of the wild west but they might be,
and I lost track of what was expected of me as curator, as visitor, as
    instigator.

JK

Art Yarn

1. JK

My maternal grandfather was an artist who was a signwriter.
On commission, and under the eye of the public, he painted
the giant Queen Elizabeth for the 1954 'Royal Visit'
and the giant Captain Cook (with map of *New Holland*)
for the 200th 'celebrations'. These lines, read on their own,
state facts. The rest of the facts are implied.
I expect implication from art. What these massive
portraits stuck up on buildings in the Terrace —
not a symbol, but the act of retaining it symbolic —
imply, beyond drawing attention to 'monumental'
occasions of imperialism, is painting as diversion.
Grandpa was highly skilled at his job. He migrated
from London at 12 in 1913 ('just before the War'),
and kept London in his head all his life. Everybody
liked Bob. His brush only did part of the talking.

2. CPG

My maternal grandfather was a station hand
He went to Perth in the 1950s, he had tuberculosis
I never heard of him doing any paintings but his
Daughter Aunty Mary was a magical bark painter
Stripping tree bark, using Indian ink and pressed flowers
Aunty created the most beautiful bark paintings
Mullewa CWA hosted her exhibition in Mullewa
Aunty was also a station house maid as a young woman
Just like her mother and older sisters were back then
Mum said they both served the Governor General out at

Minilya Station dressed in white hats and white aprons
I wonder if they had dreamt of creating art or paintings?
I wonder if they could dream of being creative in those times?

3. JK

I don't know what to do with the saying I hear sometimes
that 'art comes to you from someone else', because I wonder
which bit of art it refers to or whether it just means some
kind of skill set? Or a sensibility? A way of seeing or not
seeing? Like 'a musical family' or 'a family of writers'.
I wonder about traits of circumstance — say things people
would not claim as theirs or push aside embarrassedly
with, 'There wasn't much choice … it was just the way
things were back then …' and I think, well the way
things are now *isn't* great and I don't accept *that*
and don't want to see pictures that glorify the things
that aren't so great. But I am lucky as well because
my brother who 'got the gift' has never seen things
the way heredity would have them play out and with
skills and visions of his own devising, finds a path
through that doesn't get lost in his trying to find
himself in someone else's picture, or as they see it.
I am not saying art doesn't happen in families — it often does —
but that it doesn't have to always happen in a certain way,
or that an artist who follows another artist is necessarily
'the same' though sometimes there can be many
good reasons and needs for cultural and familial
passing down of skills and knowledge, with inflections
of difference. But colonial mindsets passing on
colonial views make no pictures I want in my head,
and the artists in the family agree. What comes out speaks.

Hey, John, I haven't heard that saying before and now
it has me thinking about what could this mean
Was it for the person who just wanted to admire others' art?
Was it for the person who felt they couldn't create art?
Is this for the Curators in the world working with creators?
Is this for the buyer wanting to decorate their homes?
Or the cashed-up collector looking for an art investment?
I know the saying 'art comes from deep within you' telling
storylines of feelings, ideas, beliefs, and connections
the storytellers exhale their inner most thoughts onto
canvas, paper, carvings, weaving using their Mara to create
the guru then sees paintings, baskets, lyrics, drawings
Is this what it means by 'art coming to you from someone else'?
A colonial mindset proudly carrying on colonial views of
the fine arts only originating from Europe is the authentic art
the oil paintings, sculptures, and the grand architecture
Is this what it means by 'art coming to you from someone else'?
the someone else meaning another culture a western one and
Aboriginal art is seen as something else altogether, different
Thank goodness that is only a colonial mindset sitting on the
museum, art gallery, and library shelves slowly gathering dust
For the exhibition walls, galleries, and private collections hold
Western Australian Aboriginal artists' creations in high regard
A few years back I walked into National Gallery Australia's
colonial room with its walls wrapped in colonial paintings and
colonial portraits and I had this overwhelming feeling of
suffocation, suppression, and my mind was painting a picture
I did not want in my head John. That room belongs elsewhere.

5. JK

I have used pieces of my brother's art for cover after cover
of my books and have copies of many pieces though many
pieces have been lost over the years and his hands are
now so broken and gnarled and swollen from decades
of shearing that he finds it hard to hold the pen or brush
so fine so particular but then he is no less fine and particular
with his handpiece that shakes the hand deeper than bone or sinews.
He cares for the sheep as he cares for the way they are drawn.
Ever since he was a small child wandering away from others
wandering away from school being called out by teachers
caned for his absence but celebrated in his family for
finding his own way to nature to the swamp to the trees
he drew the fabulous things he saw and felt and when night
drew him to the windows he drew the things he could see
that no one else could — some came down from the stars,
some from the depths of the sky, some from the tops
of trees. People said he lived in his own world, but
I knew it was part of all our world and that he could
see it and drew it so we might know some of what's there.
When I look out the window into night I see
        and know what to write.

6. CPG

I asked my sister to collaborate on a weaving piece
on which I incorporated an Abrolhos mabe pearl
I needed a locally made show off piece in Manchester
I loved the energy we both wove together on this
I have worked on large scale collaborative paintings
and wrapped decommissioned MWA antennas
from Boolardy SKA site in the Murchison with my sister's

Family hands moving together mixing of energy sharing
being in a space away from domestic issues in life
I wonder what our shearer Dad would have thought of
his daughter's artworks on paper and canvas and
yarn bombing 'spider' antennas with Australian wool
from the sheep's back into the Art Centre and our hands?
We drew the universe together and played within the
great Milky Way dreaming of collecting emu eggs
looking back on our childhoods drawing inspiration
walking in the Mullewa bush the centre of our existence
clutching a small potato and water bottle making
memories for talk in a group of artists weaving baskets
Many years later in our new homes on the coast
my writing has been a solo affair though and yet
my family have always been nearby in my thoughts

7. JK

Pencils and pastels — I sketch and smudge
into my writing journal. Words entangled
in the foliage, the rocks that try to keep
them close. I can't help thinking again
of my maternal grandfather — yes, the signwriter —
with his watercolour and sketch blocks, preparing
for another oil painting, long before I was born.

Long before. He would sit in the old
Western Australian Art Gallery for days
carefully copying — 'picture perfect',
as it's said, a canvas of the same dimensions
as the 'original', with his palette and brushes ...
and entirely absorbed as visitors stood over
his shoulder, comparing his effort with the original,

the progress of the *copy*. He seems
to have done such things
because the 'secrets' of paintings
interested him. Hans Heysen's 'Droving
Into the Light' was one he copied, and it now sits
on my aunt's loungeroom wall, with the light
of the valley boxing it in. It is a *remarkable*

piece of work in itself, and I feel his passion for 'the rules'
I don't share, and the light which is from
the 'monumental gum trees' as much as the sun
is not the light of here, and is not the light
as my grandfather understood it. I also get
that suffocating feeling in those colonial
painting rooms—maybe it's different,

but i still feel revulsion. Colonialism
is economics while ignoring — or exploiting — something
more connected, more knowledgeable of the world … colonial
economics has no knowledge worth having, to my mind.
When I was in the police lockup and court rooms time
and again in my youth, it reminded me of the art gallery's
colonial rooms — and now the old Perth Court Room

is part of the display, and that eats at my psyche.
But yes, the walls and between the walls
of the gallery as a whole can be a decolonising,
and Aboriginal art speaks and is not to be copied.
And it was in the state gallery that my son Tim as a small child
encountered Shane Pickett's 1998 'untitled' river painting
and said, with joy, 'I think I know where that is!' He wouldn't leave.

8. CPG

I tried many times to do the writing Journal
Thingy with little sketches and pretty colours
But getting so many notebook gifts mean
My words take journeys into what is visible
and within the reach of my pen and hand
Sometimes I find little word gems hidden
Away for me to find one day — little word surprises
So, I guess I never mastered the art of journalling
Into one space but across many pages of my life
Hey JK, I never heard about this copying art from
Art Gallery walls way back before our times
And I kinda have mixed feelings about it
Was that a Victorian era practice back then?
Anyways, that yarn reminded me about recently
When another poet introduced cento poetry
Practice of creating cento poems from others'
Lines, poems, verses, and written works
I had mixed feelings about that style as well
And didn't feel right doing that kind of writing
But I thought I would create a cento poem
From my own collection of poetry and I
Did just that. I wrote my very own cento poem
Drawn from eight poems in my collection
'Just Like That' and just like that cento came
Telling a story about community drinking and violence

Take the punches, hits, verbal abuse
Everyone drinks /everyone fights
Your mother was hit behind doors
Let's go find out meats /we will have a brawl
Or you might find yourself on the ground

There is the sharing of the carton
So much drinking /your body shrinking
Are the songs tucked away?
until the king browns kick in.

I wasn't surprised with the cento story it's
All part of the ongoing impact of colonisation
Just like that time I went to the Australian
National Gallery in Canberra and saw the
Colonial Room with its stiff art and predictable
Frames. I felt quite suffocated looking at
That art and the smell of concrete inside
That was heavy other people's art indeed
But I will say the Tasmanian shell necklaces
Made me forget colonial heavy art rooms

9. JK

Who gets to do the saying?
Each artwork we walk past
in the gallery that doesn't
speak to where we've ended
up is still an artwork, and
has its way of talking, and
insists on the things it has
to say, quietly, loudly, in an
offensive whisper behind
a cupped hand, with a splash
or eruption of pigment,
within and without a frame:
or just lifted by the market
out of someone's life and made

a moment to display. What

about an artwork that speaks
to community of the place
it comes from, to the place
in which it is displayed, that
says *we* will do the speaking
and it's not you speak for us,
looking on like you command
the viewing, your eyes
hungry for reward, for taking —
all proud of your position
on issues and matters,
on health and rights
and everything that's
painted in front of you
for all your claims of
being able to read it?
Who gets to do the saying.

I know this, and I write
myself out of the conversation.
I got so furious over the excuses
for capitalism that I talked over
the only reply that mattered.
I thought I was agreeing
and that agreeing was enough.
It isn't. I don't get to say,
and the shape of my letters
is an artless display
beyond the conventions
I have broken: and that's
not enough, and says too

much about it saying less,
without my keeping quiet
to listen. Paint drying?
Those lines that shape?
The significance. The makers.

Landscape Art

The problem begins
with the notion of 'outdoors' —
the separation of house-of-world
from house-as-dwelling, walls
that split horizons, that divide
hills and valleys, that sandbag
or train the river's chosen
path. As if it's a set of techniques
in rendering how it is seen
as much as conveyed, the surface
photosensitive, the 'play
of light' tweaked via levels of colour
the saturation of exposure
and the easing of vegetation
and topography into shapes
that *suggest* — as if we
were there, too, without
doors or frames in the way,
a brushing and scraping
into perspective, keeping
the ghosts out (but not
'moodiness') to prevent
it being read as *fantastical* —
sullying that ambience
of open air as paint fumes
overwhelm proportion,
distort the trained or even self-taught
eye. The problem begins
with rendering what you see.
'Authentically'?

JK

Landscape Art Response

The problem includes the
Notions of nature, outdoors
And a wilderness belonging
To a different window to view
When sitting in the same space
And dreaming of being outside
I never did like landscape art
Except for Namatjira and the
Noongar landscape art movement
But in recent years I have looked
into colonial landscapes to see what
stories existed in this type of art
For First Nations people's existence
Or did these artists paint landscapes
Just as an offering to the highest bidder
Who wanted an extra window to gaze into
There must have been some love surely
The type of love I speak of is that I see and
Hear Shane Pickett speak of through his
landscape country art when he said
"It is from the landscape that
All our culture and beliefs come"
And there is the difference for me

CPG

1967

response to Charmaine's painting High Vote of No, *2017 (see colour insert)*

'I was 5 years old living in Mullewa I don't remember the event! 13 years later in Canberra I was introduced to the 1967 Referendum. Today I know I live in an area that had a high vote for 'NO', but here we are surviving, live and proud Aboriginal people in Geraldton W.A.'

Charmaine Papertalk-Green

I was not in that area when the vote
was taken, but I would be eight
years later. Your words of connection,
tradition, ancestors and country,
painted in an area occupied by voters
who went near 30% against —
shocking but not surprising,
knowing what I would later
know. In the greater area
of dispossession, it was over 90%
in favour, but not where you were
growing with your land and people.
In the grey telling of colonial words
a negative of the colonial votes
the colonial signatures you unwrite
their white language you know better,
how its components and different lines
are made, are opened, are connected
with. You know the way through
the shapes of kinship and terrain.
You paint-write-paint-write
a poetry of telling and refusal.

The body is shaped in numbers
that are letters taken back from
the theft of time enacted by chroniclers
who followed in the supply
train of the explorers, surveyors,
administrators, assessors, military,
constabulary, shopkeepers, magistrates,
farmers, miners, governors, teachers,
tailors and seamstresses, cooks, nurses,
voters and their families. Your paint-writing
undoes and speaks outside of mapping,
of 'landscape', speaks out of country and presence.
In all my rejection of what 'Australia' is
I am caught in the way I accessed information
and the way I tried to write about it — failing —
has brought me to the point where I renounce
my efforts as an easy way out. I should have
been more forthright and just said, I have
no privileges in this. I was only four in 1967
and also don't remember. Is this telling
in its own way? I remember so much,
but not that. Was it unspoken because
it wasn't 'for children', when children
were its very essence? Wasn't for
which children? Children assimilated
into its narrative? I think I might remember —
overheard conversations,
though maybe I've been trained
to forget and am yet to unravel this
into mea culpas that fix nothing? The
way of 'talking about' falls out of date?
Different words were used in different times?
But injustice is clear as the iron mountain
the lauded miner makes disappear.

The sense of things wrong was everywhere —
the gun slits in old outbuildings, games
along the river with spears of bamboo —
always defending, as if that was our role
to hide the truth of attack, of mass murder.
Not many years later, we were learning
at school of the 'law-abiding' whites
who fought in Pinjarra, and we heard nothing
of the truth of massacre. How is this unravelled
as the words are called across the timeline?
How do kids make friends without
a way of talking this over? — they don't,
and I didn't, and I found ways in poems
but had no control over them. Control
was a problem I didn't want. I drank,
I drugged, I separated myself off.
I thank all those families who took me in
for a night here and there to see
I kept out of trouble. Nothing will undo
all that was said, and spoken. The stories
I was told I have never repeated, and won't.
The white bloke who needed *saving*
from himself, who had very little to give back.
I don't know why you all bothered with me,
but thanks, I have never forgotten. Friendship.
But even the poems went wrong, and my ironies
were lost and my training was all askew.
I clung to Blake and Shelley, and should
have forgotten them. What do the 80% lay down
as their record — acreage, profit, 'lifestyle'?
I occupied space and lived without understanding.
But I was aware. And I knew animals and birds
did not answer to the names I was told to give them.
And living in Bluff Point at fifteen I knew

that no chemistry experiments would answer
anything about what constituted the ground
the air and the sea. I lament all the internal
collapses that prevented me from finding
the best way to express what I knew.
I had no language outside the language
of houses, shops, paddocks, machines
and 'nature' obscured by rules of engagement
set in me like trade routes and 'wild outdoors'
magazines, but out on the salt scalds I knew,
and I spoke out loud, though now it seems
like something parodic, but it wasn't,
and I bled inside with heatstroke (white hot).
As the case may be. My heart bleeds.
The sound of tiny violins. All that stuff
other kids would throw back to shut me down.
Toughen up. That's the past, won't
make any difference now, mate.
Yet I knew that wasn't true.
But telling it all now is, well,
uncomfortable, and who wants
to hear? Probably no one, and this is
both a good sign as those who suffered
most are better able to be heard, and maybe
also a bad sign, because where those colonial
ways are deeply entrenched, they remain so
and won't be reached. The 'now' is only so for
those who believe in it, not for the percentage
who look back and regret justice messing
with their *false claims*, their pseudo-legacies.
But then, shifts can be deeper than I think —
a year and a half ago I was standing
by the river at 'Woodbridge' (and the 1830
farm ricochets across the stained waters)

when a couple of Elders came up
and started telling people with them
about the river and where it came from
and how it found its way to the sea,
and gradually a crowd of people
appeared and stood respectfully
and listened as the Elders continued —
generous, knowledgeable, welcoming —
and I knew then that poetry
of a healing kind, of an honest kind,
of a language beyond my ability
was forming between the people
standing there and the river,
and that its grammar was complex
and easy, while sound and sight
were walking, swimming and flying —
time being reworked or recalled.
1967, Charmaine — the government
feeling secure in its possession
of country, willing to ask 'the people'
if laws should be written, if the census
might be expanded. The gall of it all.
And my making poetry out of the same
language using the same lexicography,
means a poem created only
out of its materials
will hold back or not be able
to control truth, whether I know it
or not — those efforts made to acknowledge
disintegrating into bark, pigment, feather,
rock … or an image collected as an explorer collects,
forgetting as soon as it's handed over
to a museum. It is too easy to forget the provenance
of this language I use against official language —

it is steeped in the Aboriginal languages
the voicings of presence that resisted
and resist its grammar and namings,
that remake to undo, to reclaim.
The reflection seen in your '1967'
is not mine to be seen — I am sure
my mother would have voted 'Yes',
and likely others in my family, too,
but I, for all my unknowing
or unremembering as a small child,
would have known of language
outside the language of referendum —
the talk that ends up
inside legislation —
and started to learn how to see
and hear, to read your painting.

    JK

1967

Charmaine's painting High Vote of No, *2017, (see colour insert)*

I came to strongly believe in the rights
for Aboriginal people — my people
As a teenager in Canberra over East
The 1967 Referendum had come
And gone over a decade before
I was growing up in its shadow
Not fully aware of the significance
Teenage socialising high on agenda
But 1967 I was in Mullewa and my
Younger sister Caroline (RIP) was born
It was emu egg season so we could
Have been out looking for emu eggs?
Probably not though cause Mum was
On the committees and would have
Wanted to vote in the colonial system
That counted its sheep, wheat, and cattle
More than it did the First Nations peoples
A colonial system carrying nullius myths
Aboriginal people didn't exist and they
Definitely didn't need to be counted but
These invisible people could be used
on pastoral stations, on farms, and as
labourers to work their own country taken
from them in often cruel barbaric ways
the pre referendum language when it
came to Yamaji people included words and
thoughts such as 'invisible' 'obsolete' 'erased'
Australia a colonial space with a colonial
Constitution where Aboriginal people — Yamaji
Were not part of this introduced colonial mob

You know when you don't include a group
In your population by counting them that says
A lot about a nation — Australia own that because
Counting people just to get money from the
Federal government needs to be remembered
As part of pre referendum language despite rights

The Geraldton Guardian on 23 May 1967 wrote:
[... *there are many problems in which Commonwealth*
Aid would be invaluable — in which it is urgently
Needed. Three such aspects come to mind immediately.
Those of education, housing, and health]

The Geraldton division YES vote was 70.92%
So, there was some decent people around then
With human rights for Yamaji on their mind?
Or maybe it was seen as a tool for assimilation?
It's hard to know yet statistics tell a story, unna.
Kalgoorlie, Greenough, and Geraldton had
High NO votes holding hands and mindsets
And they still holding hands with the level of
Murders, Deaths in Custody, Police violence
And their online social media pages are eerily
Similar with hatred, violence, and threats on
our young. This is the post referendum language
we live with. This can't be ignored and made
invisible, no it can't. If that is allowed to be a
response, and a Western Australia response at that,
what story is being delivered? It's not reconciliation?
In the 1970s–80s there was a mood of change and
'fire in the Aboriginal belly' fight for rights on
all levels. The colours emerged as a symbol of
people solidarity. Aboriginal Australia was shaking
up the colonial shackles. The post 1967 Referendum

language was 'self-determination' for a long time
The infrastructure for Aboriginal services industry was laid
Although there was a mood of change
the colonial state was still in control
with money given and taken away just as fast
That Federal money talked about in the 1967 Referendum
Was controlled by walybala bureaucrats — the politician ones
Always was so the colonial shackles remained although shaken
Then another post 1967 Referendum shift came with Aboriginal
organisations closed, shut down, disappeared, funding centralised
and partnerships with walybala corporations became the norm —
they got the funding of course. I heard one of the corporates call it
decentralisation best practice crap to save money or something
Then we got all the strangers from Perth City flying in for us to help
Them to help us cause they had no community connection
See, the colonial state can tighten them shackles back up anytime
That is their money and that's what we got counted for back then
Colonial constitution, framework, population, and federal funds
I wonder when the post 1967 Referendum language shifted to
Exclude the 1967 Referendum language — is that finished now?
My community is looking a bit faded quite a few Aboriginal
Organisations have disappeared, lateral violence on rise with
Corporations fighting over the same funding bone, others have
Assimilated to keep the dollars afloat and please the funder with
A 'whole of community approach' with wide arms

I vote at all the elections — state and federal and I am
Not even sure my vote really counts. But I vote.

CPG

Everlastings (2020)

response to Charmaine's painting Wildflower in Time, *2015, (see colour insert)*

They fade quicker than we might notice,
though my grandmother — flower arranger —
hung them in bunches in dark rooms
trying to keep them true to their living lives.
I used to say, they will always look different
separated from the ground — will have something
sapped from them — but she insisted, or hoped.
As a small child, I saw the curious and overwhelmed
moving through remnant woodlands
trying to find a way into the pink-white
sweep of flowering, to be lost in their
moments, to be consumed only
by doubt. And those vast effusions
that fill the blank screen of my occupancy
are gone, or thinned, and I replace
them with ideas of paintings. And thirty
years ago when my then partner
and I picked cultivated everlastings
in a communal garden, our newborn
cribbed in the glow and rustle, desperate
for a few dollars 'extra', I could only
write of it as being inside a painting.

Roadside everlastings have been
swept aside by *widening, straightening*,
'compensating' by setting aside bush
that should have already been 'set aside'.
A classic colonial deal-making. They're stuck
looking for a different way of putting it,
a less obvious way of saying the same —

everlastings are a blink of the eye,
an inland deluge a saturation
that scalds and scores memory
so it can be scraped away in reality.
Those arguments. And by way of a seed-
packet, gardeners might strive to be authentic
to country as if giving a bit back,
consoling their greenfingered selves
with the 'display of colour'; or more
compassionately, maybe it's the everlastings
interrupting, calling them to act? Possible.
Only last year, everlastings had wild-sown
on the hill above us, and looked to make
a comeback, and as they dried to transparency
and broke, we hoped. This year none, but we wait.

    JK

Everlastings (2021)

Charmaine's painting Wildflower in Time, *2015, (see colour insert)*

I come from Yamaji wildflower people
Each year we patiently wait for wildflower arrival
After the rains kiss the earth blessing for growth
The more rain the more wildflowers we know that
They pretty ones on our ancestral lands singing
And we get so happy singing for them every cycle

In Badimaya we softly sing for that everlasting
"Gugurdung, Gugurdung make me happy inside"

We place our babies on country to be caressed
By the gentle movements of the wildflower patches
The energy of renewal and love from with the earth
Passing from country and Ancestor sand grain memories
Into the spirit of our newer and next generations
They will be forever happy to see the wildflower every year

In Wajarri we gently hum an everlasting lullaby
"Ugundungu, ugundungu, ugundungu pretty one makes me smile"

In springtime on Yamaji country a childhood of playing
Amongst the fields of pom poms, belly buttons and everlastings
Our little eyes bursting wide open from a sight that never bores us
The dry bush with its paper like trees retreat into the background
And the wildflowers come out to play like gifts from our old people
Being pushed to the surface with energy and force of many before

On Nhanagardi Wilunyu country we whisper to the winds

"Float us like flower petals into the fields of colours on uthuru"

Teenage Yamaji goddesses draping wildflowers like sparkling
Jewels necklaces and earrings linked together to adorn our teenage bodies
Bounty from an earthly treasure chest tucked away safely within country
An offering from generations before as a reminder of spiritual beauty
Around our graceful feet we wear flower footwear while still being
Connected and feeling the pulse of country connecting forever

In Wajarri our spirit shouts out our happiness at such beauty
"Julgarra, julgarra, julgarra, beauty rich in our wildflower ones"

Yamaji mother looking through the window at the rain clouds
The washing won't get done today but that's ok, the flowers are
Waiting to return for their annual visit to bring childhood memories
Of happiness when seeing flower gifts being pushed through the grounds
From the hands of many ancestors, grandmothers, old grandmothers
The women's business for strength never fades like wildflowers never fades.

In Badimaya we sing wildflower song of falling in love, wildflower love
"Gudurdu yuga — falling in love — Gugurdung — wildflower"

In springtime in wildflower season time Yamaji flower time is our time
We feel proud of our country and how it can make the world smile
The marlu eat the wildflowers offering Yamaji a delicious feed like
A wildflower gifting itself to its living relatives strengthen bond forever.

CPG

Shane Pickett Opened the Eyes by Our Closing Them — on his 'Untitled' (1998) Synthetic Polymer Paint on Canvas Painting in the Western Australian Art Gallery

I said to young Tim
who was overwhelmed
by the river with kangaroo paws
and pelicans as it swirled about
the river island, through a city of bush
before the city of Perth invaded.
And I said, stare at it, let it in,
then snap your eyes shut
like a camera, then do it again
and again studying different
parts of the painting — up close
then stepping back to take it all in
but take nothing away from it,
provide no captions, let it sing.
The same and yet different. Nothing
is the same now and everything
is the same and different. The pelicans
wingbeat in time with currents
however much they've been
messed with. Fabulous
and yet real as real can be —
a truer geography than sold
at school, in the Department
of Planning, Lands and Heritage.
Yes, and the blue in the air,
and the yellow pollen,
and the sun-pink glister
of the waters. Yes.

And now an adult, he says
to me, Do you remember
when you showed me that Shane
Pickett painting of the river
in the art gallery, and said to see
it more intensely through 'photoing'
in my head? Taking nothing,
but seeing more in letting *it*
paint its way in? Yes. Well,
I remember every part of it,
he says, and see it many times over
still. 'Untitled', yet the river
we would know — down
through the hills which we cross
when entering the city,
still questioning our senses,
trying to learn how to
see through the buildings,
follow the pelicans.

JK

Ngana Nyinda? Who Are You?

commissioned work for 'Who Are You: Australian Portraiture',
National Gallery of Victoria, 2022

Bringing together my bundle of kangaroo skin, emu feathers, kangaroo
sinew, quandong and bush seeds. To stitch a woman's story of women
storytellers. A story of First Nation women storytellers. Women
narratives of hands, eyes, energy, culture, identity, colonisation,
decolonising, and a long line of ancestors.

But now let me whisper call out to my grandmothers:
"Nyarlu Jugarnu ... Aba ... Gantharri"

The line of Grandmothers has called out to these women to pass on
stories through their hands, eyes, and energy. To break the glass ceilings
of stereotypes when replying to "who are you?" I tread gently in this
story through and in the space of time, place and peoples, First Nations
peoples, Women. Holding hands sharing energy sharing connection to
Ancestors, culture, and country. Looking back if we must but remember
the past is with us and being carried forward in our ideas, our actions,
our thoughts, our memories, our cultural practices, our customs, our
knowledge, and our cultural identity. Through nyarlu eyes, nyarlu
hands, nyarlu energy, and nyarlu knowing we survive.

I. A RESPONSE TO 'MRS WOODS AND 'ERE' (2013) BY KARLA DICKENS

> Ngana Nyinda — Who Are You?
> I am the face of many communities
> I am the keeper of many knowledges
> My head is wrapped in an outer scarf of
> Generational trauma, sorrow, and grief
> But I am protected by deep culture
> I am the grandmother you seek within

2. A RESPONSE TO 'POSSUM SKIN CLOAK' (2020) BY MAREE CLARKE

Ngana Nyinda — Who Are You?
I am the gift of warmth and beauty
I am the grandmother in your dreams
I whisper amongst many about our old ways
You captured my whisper and with your hands
Stitched together our cultural practices
Nothing is ever lost but found to those who listen

3. A RESPONSE TO 'MAGIC WEAVER' (2005) BY YVONNE KOOLMATRIE

Ngana Nyinda — Who Are You?
I am the magic weaver forever binding together
The water, air, land, salt, soil, wind, and grasses
We women are woven together from every ancestor
I am bound to my country and my country to me
I am the grandmother within every cell of your being

4. A RESPONSE TO 'NGALIM-NGALIMBOOROO NGAGINBE' (2019) BY SHIRLEY PURDIE

Ngana Nyinda — Who Are You?
I am the woman artists in many First Nation art centres
Painting stories to be transmitted to our families
From connection to a full moon and daughter tree
From touching the earth of country, memory, and story
From taking the gift of cultural knowledge to the canvas
I am grandmothers' memory and culture holder for tomorrow

5. A RESPONSE TO 'SELF PORTRAIT' (1999/2005) BY TRACEY MOFFATT

Ngana Nyinda — Who Are You?
I am the eye storyteller showing myself to you
I can create and change narratives from the
Black and white of life with instructions through
To the rosy cheeks of a hand-coloured stereotype breaker
I am many grandmothers many eyes seeing and seeing
awakening narratives by looking to the distant future

6. A RESPONSE TO 'WARRIOR WITHOUT A WEAPON' (2019) BY NAOMI HOBSON

Ngana Nyinda — Who Are You?
I am every grandmother grandson of ancestral country
First Nation men nurtured through maternal love
In each campsite before a manhood life journey
I am as gentle as the sweet breeze and soft grass
My tears are carried within each trauma seen or felt
I am grandmothers' sons, grandsons, and great grandsons

7. A RESPONSE TO 'OPPRESSION, REPRESSION (FAMILY PORTRAIT)' (2004) BY YHONNIE SCARCE

Ngana Nyinda — Who Are You?
I am the First Nations Families that could not
Be oppressed, repressed, or written out of history
I am the love of family treasured down the generations
I am family strength rising from each heartbeat
Our family portraits remind this country we survived
I am the grandmothers' seeds protected to flourish

8. A RESPONSE TO 'FEDERATION SERIES 1901–2001' (2001)
   BY JULIE DOWLING

> Ngana Nyinda — Who Are You?
> I am the many Yamaji faces seen within
> the history archives of this intercultural space
> I am the First Nation faces of the many
> Narratives endured since colonisation
> I am the storyteller painting each face giving each
> narrative a face because our stories have never been faceless

9. A RESPONSE TO 'MATILDA (NGAMBRI/NGUNNAWAL)' (2020)
   BY BRENDA CROFT

> Ngana Nyinda — Who Are You?
> I am the First Nations women who fight for the
> Rights of their people by being visible and with a voice
> In their communities and advocating in the corridors
> Of Parliament houses and governments around Australia
> I am First Nation women radiating a staunch proud identity
> I am grandmothers' granddaughters keeping inside fire alive

> *But now let me whisper call out to my grandmothers:*
> *"Nyarlu Jugarnu … Aba … Gantharri"*

CPG

Yagu and Gadja

A Response to 'Mother and Baby (Passage Series)' from Tracey Moffatt's My Horizon,
Venice Biennale Australian Pavilion, Italy (2017)

The fog can bring images
Of spirits for one to see
I see these of the past
On the mother's face
Making themselves known
For a reason that you
Must be able to read
To be able to understand
Looking through and looking out
If it's a portal you seek?
Then here it is for you
A reminder of before
A warning of the future
Her face has not disappeared
The old people are simply
Borrowing the space
For they know you
Will stare into mother
Wanting to caress her skin
The fog brings images
Of spirits for the baby
For there are things
Only a baby or child will see
Passages to a new time
To a new existence
Or maybe your inner child
Yearning for what was missed
Old Aunty said watch out for fog

For it brings spirits under cover
This is a time to be careful

    CPG

Yagu means 'mother' in Wajarri, Gadja means 'baby' in Wajarri

Touching both

A Response to 'Touch (Body Remembers Series)' from Tracey Moffatt's My Horizon,
Venice Biennale Australian Pavilion, Italy (2017)

Man-made stone cave
For another's purpose
They have long gone
I watch how you embrace
You touch and you cling
Your skin to stone and rock
Connecting to something
Or someone who touched
This same space long ago
For that moment you are
Reluctant to peep around
The corner to what could
Be waiting or what is not
You are not that woman
That house help from back
For your hair is styled
Your fingernails to clean
Your elegance of body
From softer work done
You do not know that
Hard work of station life
For the generations later
Where freed of this slavery
Crying and nestling into
A space where your
Grandmother softly whispers
From within this hardened earth

"Don't forget me my granddaughter"
And you have not forgotten

CPG

Retracing Steps of a Morning Meeting in Late Afternoon

for C & T

The ship's horn sounds twice as it leaves the port,
tugs letting go, and the osprey draws sea, sand and spinifex
    into the departure — a yellow honeyeater is quick
near the beach and a 'foreshore' rejects its description.

Where the littoral stonework holds a slow sea
as long as it can — bowl, font, cradle, scoop, cup, sluice —
weed sweeps through making liquid static. We heard
of a family making art together today, and in that art

the patterns we can't describe so easily, not knowing
what's to come of what we see and put down in lines
and curves, the swirls from a diving cormorant, the sweep
of shore that only partly comes from the departing ship.

'St George's Beach' is where we meet and talk it all over —
but the name doesn't do anyone justice, and its governance
    serves no ideas of this space, no long-learned truths,
no communities working their ways of sea and stone, sand and air.

JK

Appendix: Interview with Trevor Pickett by Charmaine

Geraldton Regional Art Gallery, on the morning of 11 September 2021

CPG: This is Charmaine Green, talking with Trevor Pickett. I wanted to yarn with Trevor so he can give us some insight from a family perspective and from an artist's perspective on his dad's works. If you'd like to introduce yourself first, Trevor.

TP: Yeah, good day, I am Trevor Pickett. I'm the youngest son of Shane. There was two of us, myself and my brother, Roger. Yeah, I'm 39 now, Dad passed in 2010, so it's been 11 years since he passed. Yeah, grew up in Perth, me as well, mostly around Balga. Then had the kids in Golden Bay just next to Secret Harbour, and we lived there for seven years.

CPG: From what you know, what were your dad's greatest influences? Was Albert Namatjira an early one?

TP: He never actually said whether Namatjira was, but you could just see in the artwork. His first early styles were those landscapes, but Dad always had that passion for country, for the colours. He was doing his own colour palettes and stuff.

CPG: When you're saying he had the passion for country, did he often return to where he grew up?

TP: Yeah, yeah, he took us out there a few times. We go out you know, where Nanna and Pop were, Tammin, Quairading, where they were living in their times. Midland when they were out there, too. He did take us out to the Old Reserve, you know, where they used to live, where they had their little shacks when they were kids.

CPG: And were the stories of his family woven into his paintings?

TP: Well, it's a tough one. I can't say whether he said it at the time. Yeah, more so in his later works, which are more abstract type ones which were predominantly about the song lines of our country, where everything travels and works together, and you can see where they cross, you know, the edge of the borders, of our land boundaries.

CPG: The six seasons were very much part of his later painting cycle. Did he paint according to the seasons?

TP: As far as making combinations with the colours, I can't say he would, but I guess most of his works were commissioned stuff. So, you just paint to what people wanted and you're selling them mostly.

CPG: They did that really large painting on the Noongar six seasons, do you recall that painting at all?

TP: Is that the one where they were all working together, collaboration with the whole group of big artists and that? I haven't seen it in person myself. Because during that time I was in mining, and I was away for quite a while, I was doing longer swings then.

CPG: So, you're doing other things. Have you explored his relationship with the paintings and his ancestors?

TP: He always had that story behind his works, that he wasn't just putting paint on there because it looks good. He always made a connection somewhere along the lines in it and you could see it. Cause he had arthritis since he was little, towards the end now he struggled a lot to hold paintbrushes, and so he'd make his own brushes with bigger handles or broomsticks even.

CPG: Really broomstick?

TP: Yeah, big broomstick handles, putting stuff on the end of it to use them with the paint. I've got a pretty big painting at home and you can see his hand work where he was using gloves, you know, so you can see his actual hand work in there in the paint.

CPG: I went into the Subiaco studio when he was in there. He invited me back into his studio space. I was amazed at all the different sized canvases he was working on in one time and then he said, "Come here, I want to show you something". He put on gloves and showed me how he was putting the paint on the canvas.

TP: I think that's why I like the painting at home because I can see his hands in it and, you know, I guess that's my connection to Dad. He is still there.

CPG: When you talked about using a broom, my mind went to him brushing the country like sweeping the country with this broom, but on a canvas.

TP: He was good with whatever he did. He was probably one of the cleanest painters they've ever known because he always come home with his clothes. Look still clean, no paint spilt on them, nothing.

CPG: But he did these incredible big paintings.

TP: Yep, all day painting.

CPG: Now your dad spoke of art as healing. Is there anything that you could pick up from there? Because even just our talking now with seeing his hand marks on a canvas, there's part of healing as well.

TP: He was always talking about cultural healing and how it is important to us. Most of the later works he did were for hospitals, you know, and I think there's in the new children's hospital, what's that one? Is that Fiona

CPG: Stanley? Yeah.

TP: Well, there's stuff in Fiona Stanley [Hospital].

CPG: There's stuff of his everywhere in the courthouse too.

TP: The courthouse ones are really good. There was a funny story about that one. So you've got the normal courthouse and then you got the one that's the opposite, at the High Court House?

CPG: There's a federal court, and there's a big one in Perth on Hay Street.

TP: They're both opposite each other.

CPG: Yeah.

TP: So, in one there is that big, big swan?

CPG: Yeah, that's the one, right?

TP: Yeah, that piece was huge, and they only wanted a painting from an Indigenous artist. And the price for that wasn't massive but then in the other courthouse, the section they wanted an artwork for was not as big, not even half of that size, but the price was almost double. Because it was open to everyone else. And Dad was saying, you know, that's the system trying to help white people more. But he's like, I won it so, you know, stick it to the man.

CPG: But you know, the artwork in the courthouse is massive. What's it called, The Swan River? I've been in there a couple of times, I've got told off from trying to take a photo so I can write about it, I've got hunted out of there for doing that. The massive size of those paintings, and them being placed in those spaces, that's kind of a healing thing in itself that your dad would be really happy to see.

TP: He was always happy as long as an Aboriginal artist wins. Whether it be himself or someone else, someone else upcoming, whatever.

CPG: Was there a painting in particular that shows his transition from being a realist painter? I think that means from the landscapes to a more abstract kind of work. But abstract is also a word for something that might, in fact, be its own kind of realism.

TP: From the early landscapes, yes, they stood out on their own — then I do remember him getting more into oils. He did the Rainbow Serpent (The Waygl) and the willy wagtail man, which is more our cultural style. Yeah, telling the stories, they're not really realism. Or are they? But the detail of the animals, I guess you could say that's realist, but just from that oil. Then he went back to doing landscapes again, but he added a bit of a spiritual touch to the landscapes, the abstract song lines and stories. There wasn't really a clear transition between the two. He did those acrylics, pouring for a little while, but then there were really detailed animals on top of that. Where did the transition between the two start?

CPG: Yeah, in those larger, more abstract ones you can see country. You can see a whole lot of things in it, and then you see the song line coming through. What was happening around that time?

TP: In life, I think he was probably a bit more cultural at that time.

CPG: What's that mean?

TP: You know, in that way, he went through.

CPG: Oh, okay. Yeah, sorry. Yeah.

TP: Yeah. So, at that time, so you could see the difference. You know, he had his eyes opened.

CPG: So, he was seeing and giving in a different way then. What do you reckon his relationship was between making his artwork and the Dreaming?

TP: He's name Meeyakba, you know, Meeyakba, that's his bush name. Which I think Pop said means soft light of the moon. But everyone just called Dad Shiny Moon, you know, all the family. So that's probably the white way of saying Shiny Moon easier than Meeyakba (Soft Light of the Moon).

CPG: Do your family use the Aboriginal Noongar name much?

TP: Mum doesn't like to, but Mum grew up Christian, you know? Her father and his siblings were all part of that Stolen Gen. So, she grew up in the Christian ...

CPG: Yeah, in the Christian way of thinking.

TP: Yeah, church life, church way. But even still on Dad's side, Pop was the main one that really used the name and even some of the uncles I know from Barry McGuire, he speaks language pretty well.

CPG: Do you incorporate that into your artwork or your photography or the way you look at things?

TP: I may not see the actual song lines properly, but I can see lines that you know where they actually connect and join, and I try and put that into some of my work.

CPG: Were your Dad's totems always part of his work?

TP: He always imprinted a little signature piece in the art, hidden little touches that you knew that was his.

CPG: So he put hidden messages in that family would always know and maybe someone who studied a lot closer.

TP: And he was always respectful to wherever he was. He went to Arnhem Land a few times and studied with all them mob, learning of them, and they were all helping him in his art. And you know, permission wise, you always go "You don't just walk straight up and open the fridge. You go and you ask, Is that cool? Is that right?" This is probably more when he was in that end of his landscape stuff and they loved his landscape style, whereas they were more dot painting, you know?

CPG: Did he ever use materials taken from specific sites on country that were special to him?

TP: No, I don't think he ever took anything as far as to put on the canvas like to put on the artwork. He might have used some of the sticks to help with his work. That he turned into brushes of some sort.

CPG: What were his very first artworks, and did he ever show them to others or to the family first?

TP: There was always that story Mum and my uncles and aunts tell, they said Dad did that first one in school, in primary school, just a sketching of a horse, and it was a full detail that the school wanted to buy off him, you know, it was near perfect.

He would have been early teens maybe or even younger. There was one that I saw that was really, really old, of a cottage, just a little cottage building, right? That was probably the earliest one that I've seen. I think it was in the 70s.

CPG: Where would those paintings be now?

TP: I think someone donated it to Mum and us. So, Mum's probably got that somewhere. We've got a whole collection of Dad's works from the various stages of his life, all the different styles. So we can still tell the story. As we grow up, my kids can look at them and think, Oh, you can see how that changed in his artwork.

He was always changing, too. I think that was one of the things as well that contributed to him changing his styles was when someone else would do the same thing or start, you know, painting very similar to his. He'd never go off at them about copying his work. As we got older, we would ask him "Why don't you say something? Why don't you chip them for copying you? That's copyright, you know". He'd always say, "Nah, if they learned from me, well, then that's fine, because then I can see my work in their work".

CPG: He didn't mind that he was a teacher in a different way. He was sharing technique, sharing story and developing people to open their eyes to their art. Do you reckon that's a fair thing to say?

When he was painting, did he talk to you much about what he was painting? Or was it a private affair done away from everyone and then came back?

TP: Most of it was done away at his work or studio. There was a couple of times where he was teaching at my school, where he would be the art teacher or artist in residence, he'd come in and do a bit of watercolour work with us. And, you know, he's always joking and laughing as he's painting. So, he did mention you always got to have that right attitude for it, happy space, you know, don't paint in anger.

CPG: Did he ever talk about the landscape as being colonial imposition on country?

TP: Nah I can't say he did. I couldn't really see influence in those landscapes, either.

CPG: What was his relationship with other Australian artists of his time?

TP: He was always open to other artists coming in, talking to him and showing off their work and showing off his works. I think there were a couple of exhibitions where they had joint artists. I think his works and old Irwin Lewis's (dec) works were hanging at the same time. Irwin was a Yamaji man.

CPG: What did he consider his ultimate purpose for painting? Why was he painting?

TP: I think Dad was more for Blackfellas, keeping us and our spirits alive and letting the world know; his artwork, that was his way of saying we haven't lost culture. We still here, especially us Noongar being on, I guess, metro, you know. He spoke to the colonial impact, the idea that we don't have culture. Plenty of them Noongar speak language, and even young fellas speak pretty fluent language these days in Perth. This is in the city where, you know, supposed to be

CPG: Urbanised.

TP: Urbanised, that's the word. So, he was always happy to broadcast that and even some of his speeches after winning awards, he'd still remind them that's the case.

CPG: Did your dad ever talk about the wheat belt? Do you talk about the wheat belt as a region or an idea rather than, you know, like Noongar Boodjar? What are you, Balladong?

TP: Yeah Balladong. I can't say I've ever really heard him use that word Wheat Belt. Just 'going back home'. Going back Quairading way.

CPG: Going back country. So that's kind of like a farmer's or settler's way of thinking.

TP: No wheat belt. Even like driving for funerals from up here in Geraldton to Quairading the first time when my first cousin passed, we went inland way through Northam and you could just see the difference in the country. Once you get back on Noongar, country change. You can see it. And I pointed out to Justine especially when you get a bit more inland again, the trees will just change, big trees.

CPG: We've spoken about how painting is healing, and how art itself can be healing for the maker and the viewer.

TP: I guess I find photography healing. Even when I was painting for a while in my early days, I thought it is good, it's relaxing. You can't go wrong. If I was out on the country with no shoes on, just walking in the dirt and taking photos, it's even better. I love being at the beach because I like walking along barefoot. Take photos, especially to get those hard shots. Even lay on the beach.

I think one of the things that I found most interesting would have been Dad's last piece, that big art sculpture, 'Canopy' at Champion Lakes. I was a diesel mechanic working away, doing all right. Mum was like, I need your help with your father. So I left mining, come home. I was just driving Dad back and forth to a lot of his appointments, his art stuff. I think the second time I went to the sculpturist, the metalworker, Dad introduced me and the second time he said, "Oh, so if anything needs to change, you know, in my artwork, ring Trevor and speak to Trevor, because he knows what I want, and he knows more". With me being a diesel mechanic, knowing a little bit of welding, he thinks, "he knows more about metal than I do, so talk to him". Not even a week after that Dad passed away. So that was the last conversation I had with the artist, was pretty much Dad saying that's Trevor's job now.

It's almost like he knew that something might have been happening, but he wanted to make sure that his work was still his work and the way he wanted it. That was emotionally trying for me, seeing the first cut out of the metal piece, to see it up knowing Dad wasn't there to see it too. All these things that he wanted to know. Other artists have even said the same thing, you can see what he wrote on their plaque about it. You see in the work that's what he wanted.

Author biographies

Charmaine Papertalk Green was born at Eradu (between Geraldton and Mullewa) on Yamaji country. She is a member of the Wajarri, Badimaya and Nhanagardi Wilunyu cultural groups of Yamaji Nation in Western Australia. Charmaine is a visual artist, poet and writer and began writing poetry in Mullewa in the late 1970s. She was instrumental in the incubation of the nationally and internationally touring exhibition *Ilgarijiri – Things Belonging to the Sky*, a Yamaji Art collaboration with the Curtin Institute of Radio Astronomy, Curtin University, Square Kilometre Array (SKA) project, the Australian Government and City of Greater Geraldton.

Her publications include *Just Like That* (Fremantle Arts Centre Press 2007); *Tiptoeing Tod the Tracker* (Oxford University Press 2014); *False Claims of Colonial Thieves* in collaboration with WA poet John Kinsella (Magabala Books 2018); *Nganajungu Yagu* (Cordite Publishing Inc. 2019); and numerous anthologies and other publications. Charmaine was shortlisted for the Adelaide Festival John Bray Award 2020 and the ALS Gold Medal 2019 for *False Claims of Colonial Thieves*. She won the Victorian Premier's Literary Awards 2020 poetry category, won the Australian Literature Society Gold Medal (2020), and was shortlisted for the 2020 Queensland Premier's Literary Award Judith Wright Calanthe Award for *Nganajungu Yagu*.

Charmaine lives in Geraldton, Western Australia.

John Kinsella is a non-Indigenous collaborator and the author of over thirty books. His many awards include the Australian Prime Minister's Literary Award for Poetry, the Victorian Premier's Award for Poetry, the John Bray Award for Poetry, the Judith Wright Calanthe Award for Poetry and the Western Australian Premier's Award for Poetry (three times). His recent works include *The Ascension of Sheep: Collected Poems Volume One (1980–2005)* (UWAP 2022), *Drowning in Wheat: Selected Poems* (Picador 2016) and *On the Outskirts* (UQP 2017). Recent story collections include *Crow's Breath* (Transit Lounge 2015) and *Pushing Back* (Transit Lounge 2021) and a recent critical volume is *Polysituatedness* (Manchester University Press 2017). With Tracy Ryan he is the co-editor of *The Fremantle Press Anthology of Western Australian Poetry* (2017). He is a Fellow of Churchill College Cambridge University and Emeritus Professor of Literature and Environment at Curtin University, Western Australia. He lives on Ballardong Noongar land at Jam Tree Gully in the Western Australian wheatbelt and went to high school on Yamaji land in Geraldton.

Acknowledgements

Thanks to Violet Pickett, Anna Haebich, Rachel Bin Salleh and Magabala Books. Special thanks to Arlie Alizzi for all editorial input. Thanks to the Red Room (whose Poetry Month team commissioned 'Indexing'). Thanks to my family, and to Charmaine and her family. Very special thanks to Kim Scott, and Jeanine Leane for their generosity and assistance in the process of consultation.

I acknowledge that I live and work on stolen Noongar country, and that I have lived and worked on stolen Yamaji country. I am committed to the full return of country to its peoples, and further acknowledge that it was never ceded.

John Kinsella

Thanks and acknowledgement to my sons Mark and Tamati, my partner Tom, and all my family, colleagues and friends for their continued support. Thanks to John Kinsella, Edith Cowan University, University of Western Australia, First Nations Australia Writers Network, Yamaji Art Centre Geraldton, WACRH, Lowitja Institute and all my incredible colleagues in the Aboriginal Arts industry. Thanks to the late Shane Pickett's family for their support, Rachel Bin Salleh and Arlie Alizzi for their commitment, copyediting and assistance, and a special thanks to Magabala Books.

Charmaine Papertalk Green